Colophon

©Mathias Jansson (2025)

"From Mods to Museums: An Introduction to Game Art - Video Games as Contemporary Artistic Practice"

ISBN: 978-91-86915-81-0

Published by:

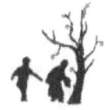 "jag behöver inget förlag"

c/o Mathias Jansson

Tvärvägen 23

232 52 Åkarp

SWEDEN

http://mathiasjansson72.blogspot.se/

Print: Lulu.com

Disclaimer: This book is written with help of ChatGPT. The author has previously conducted extensive research on the subject and has also contributed with texts about Game Art in anthologies and journals. The essays have been improved, edited and proofread by the author before publishing.

1

Table of contents

The Game Art Terminology 7

What Counts as Game Art? 9

Game Art or game art? 9

Video games and Art 10

Game Art- an established category 11

Art Mods in the 1990s: Video Games as a Medium for Contemporary Art.. 13

Play, Creativity, and the Origins of Games 13

The birth of video games.. 14

The Demoscene.. 15

The Rise of Game Modding 16

Digital and Conceptual Art Influences......................... 17

Early Art Mods 19

ArsDoom (1995) – Orhan Kipcak and Team.................. 19

Museum Meltdown Series (1996–1999) – Palle Torsson & Tobias Bernstrup.. 19

Jodi (Untitled Game, 1996–2001) 20

First Museum Shooter 20

Deconstruction of Gameplay.. 22

From Hacking to Activism.. 23

Online gaming and communities 23

Velvet-Strike and the Turn Toward Political Art 23

Joseph DeLappe: *dead-in-iraq* 24
A New Generation of Game Engines 25
The exhibition: Synreal – The Unreal Modification 26
Reception of Art Mods 28
The end of an era 30
The Museum Under Fire: From ArsDoom to Climate Activism 32
DOOM and the Birth of the First-Person Shooter 33
Technical and Cultural Innovation 34
Defining the FPS Genre 34
The Legacy of DOOM 35
ArsDoom: The First Museum Shooter (1995) 36
Museum Meltdown: The Museum Under Siege (1996-99) 37
Quake Hamburger Kunsthalle Reconstruction (1999) . 39
Stephen Honegger & Anthony Hunt's Container (2002) 40
Chris Reilly's SAIC Half-Life 2 Project (2006) 41
Paul Steen's Art Assault (2010) 43
Michiel van der Zanden's Pwned Paintings #2 (2008) .. 44
Jeff Koons Must Die!!! (2011) 46
The Tradition of Destroying Art: From Performance to Protest 47

The Continued Relevance of DOOM Modding in Museums and Contemporary Art 50

Conclusion 51

Playing with Failure: Glitch, Deconstruction, and Art in Video Games 53

Postmodern Deconstruction as Method 54

JODI *Untitled Game* (1996–2001) 55

Joan Leandre *Retroyou* series (1999–2003) 55

Cory Arcangel *Super Mario Clouds* (2002 56

Vuk Ćosić *The ASCII Unreal* (1999) 56

The History and Concept of Glitch Art 57

Rosa Menkman Glitch Moment(um) (2011) 58

Connection to Deconstructive Game Art and Art Mods 58

From Streets to Screens: Performance Art and Online Worlds 60

Antoinette LaFarge and the Plaintext Players 61

Joseph DeLappe: Nonviolence, Memory, and Digital Activism 62

COLL.EO: Performance as Digital Reenactment 63

From the Physical Body to the Virtual Avatar 64

Second Life and Synthetic Performance 65

The Sims, Parody, and Virtual Lives 70

Rainey Straus and Katherine Isbister's *SimBee* (2004.. 70

Caleb Larsen's Simulacrum (2005) 71

Angela Washko Free Will Mode (2013) 71

Mark Beasley's Vito Acconci (The Video Game) (2007) 73

Pippin Barr's The Artist is Present (2011) 73

Conclusion 74

Mike Builds a Shelter and Nuclear Games 76

Mike Builds a Shelter 76

Gameplay and Concept 77

Artistic and Cultural Significance 77

Legacy and Restoration 77

Artist and video games in the 1980s 78

Concept and Gameplay 78

Artistic and Political Context 78

Gameplay and Mechanics 79

Theatre Europe 80

WarGames 80

Legacy and Impact 81

War, Refugees, and Videogames: From Space Invaders to Contemporary Artistic Interventions 83

Joseph DeLappe's "dead-in-iraq" (2006–2011) 84

Velvet Strike (2002–2003) 85

Eddo Stern's Vietnam Romance (2003) 86

Contemporary Conflicts: Ukraine and Palestine 87

Total Refusal How to Disappear (2020) 87

Rasheed Abueideh's Liyla and the Shadows of War (2016) 88

Refugees, Borders, and Video Games 89

Escape from Woomera (2003) 89

Darfur is Dying (2006) 90

Italiani Brava Gente (1996) 90

Conclusion 91

Game Art Exhibitions a summary 92

Reference books about Game Art 95

The Game Art Terminology

The term *Game Art* emerged in the late 1990s and early 2000s as a way to describe contemporary artistic practices that draw upon videogames as subject matter, medium, or cultural reference. While artists had engaged with digital games earlier, the consolidation of "Game Art" as a category reflected the growing recognition of videogames as a cultural form worthy of critical and aesthetic exploration within the art world. The term has been used in exhibitions, academic writing, and curatorial projects to highlight the intersection between visual art and gaming culture.

Game Art can take many different forms. Some artists appropriate existing games through modifications (*art mods*), machinima, or interventions in game environments. Others create new works that mimic game aesthetics, user interfaces, or the logic of gameplay without being fully functional games. A third strand of Game Art is more conceptual, reflecting on the role of games in society, their economies, and their influence on human behavior.

Today, Game Art encompasses a wide range of practices, from artists like Cory Arcangel, Eddo Stern, and JODI who directly intervene in game code and aesthetics, to others who use gaming as metaphor or visual inspiration. What unites these practices is not a single style but the recognition of video games as one of the defining cultural technologies of the contemporary era. In this sense, Game Art functions both as an art historical category and as a lens through which to examine the impact of digital play on visual culture.

In the influential anthology *GameScenes: Art in the Age of Videogames* (2006), Italian artist, writer, and curator Matteo Bittanti—together with Domenico Quaranta—offers one of the most widely cited definitions of *Game Art*. Bittanti describes it as:

> "Any art in which video games played a significant role in the creation, production, and/or display of the artwork. The resulting work can exist as a game, painting, photograph, sound, animation, video, performance, or gallery installation."

This definition underscores two key ideas: first, that video games need not be the final form of the artwork but can function as a medium, tool, or conceptual framework; and second, that Game Art is medium-agnostic, encompassing everything from interactive works to static images and performances.

The book itself became a cornerstone in the academic and curatorial discourse on Game Art. It features essays, interviews, and critical texts alongside a rich selection of artworks by international artists who engage with video games as cultural material. GameScenes does not limit itself to playable art games; it also includes machinima, in-game photography, mods, installations, and conceptual works, mapping the diverse strategies artists employ to interrogate gaming culture. By doing so, it situates Game Art within the broader context of contemporary media art and visual culture, bridging the gap between game studies and art history.

What Counts as Game Art?

While definitions vary, most overviews converge on practice rather than essence. Categories that recur include:

- **Art mods & appropriations**: altering or re-contextualizing existing games to critique mechanics, politics, or representation.
- **Machinima**: cinematic works produced inside game engines, treated as an artistic moving-image practice in its own right.
- **Art games**: playable works authored with artistic intent, often foregrounding systems over spectacle.
- **In-game performance and installation**: actions staged within virtual worlds, sometimes documented as video or photography; exhibitions surveyed "game-related art" across such modes.

Together, these practices explain both why the term *Game Art* proved useful and why it remains contested: it spans formats (video, installation, code), sites (gallery, browser, server), and strategies (appropriation, original creation, social performance).

Game Art or game art?

In the commercial game industry, game art typically means the production graphics for a videogame—concept art, 2D/3D assets, textures, animation, UI. As Wikipedia's overview puts it, *"Game art design is a subset of game development involving the process of creating the artistic aspects of video games."* Trade glossaries likewise address palettes, shaders, pipelines, and toolchains. This is a legitimate, highly skilled design practice—but it is not what curators and scholars mean by Game Art when discussing contemporary art.

Because the same words denote two different worlds, misreadings proliferate: a gallery exhibition of critical mods might be mistaken for an art book of concept sketches, or a studio's environment art might be assumed to carry institutional claims to art-world status.

Video games and Art

Another term that has been used is *"Videogames and Art,"* as in the title of an important book in the field from 2007 by Andy Clarke and Grethe Mitchell. The combination videogame and art could also be found in exhibitions and articles. However, this phrasing carries also a certain risk of confusion. It can easily be interpreted as a contribution to the long-standing debate about whether videogames should be considered an art form in themselves. In contrast, the intention of many artists and scholars working under the term is not primarily to argue for the artistic status of games, but rather to explore how videogames function as a source of inspiration, material, or cultural reference point within contemporary art practices. The difference may seem subtle, but it is crucial: one discussion centers on legitimizing games as an autonomous art form, while the other addresses the ways in which artists appropriate, reinterpret, and critically engage with the medium of videogames in their own work.

Game Art- an established category

I have personally used the term *Game Art* since I first began writing about artists inspired by videogames. However, in recent years I have realized that there is a problem with the term, since the videogame industry usage has gained increasing ground as videogames have become more popular. Today, internet searches for *Game Art* primarily lead to material related to conceptual graphics and design for commercial videogames. Because *Game Art* within the art world is already a very small subgenre, I see a need to clarify its meaning in order to avoid confusion between these two contexts.

But the term *Game Art* has been part of the New Media Art vocabulary for more than two decades. Since the late 1990s, it has appeared in exhibitions, academic anthologies, and curatorial discourse, making it an established category within the field. Like other subgenres of New Media Art—such as Net Art, Software Art, or Bio Art—Game Art signals a practice rooted in a specific technological and cultural context: the world of video games.

Because of this long-standing usage, replacing the term entirely is neither practical nor desirable. It has historical weight and connects to a body of literature, and art). Abandoning it would risk erasing that lineage.

However, *Game Art* is a broad and sometimes ambiguous label. It encompasses everything from art mods and machinima to in-game performances, playable art games, conceptual installations and paintings. This diversity can obscure the specific strategies and intentions behind individual works.

For this reason, it is better to retain Game Art as the overarching term—just as we do with "Net Art" or "Software Art"—but adopt subgenre labels when discussing particular practices. Terms like:

- **Art Mods** – for works that modify existing games
- **Machinima** – for cinematic works created in game engines
- **Art Games** – for playable works designed as art
- **In-Game Performance** – for performative actions in virtual worlds

Using these subcategories and others provides clarity, honors the historical framework of New Media Art, and avoids the confusion that arises when trying to invent a completely new term for a well-established field.

Art Mods in the 1990s: Video Games as a Medium for Contemporary Art

The 1990s witnessed a unique convergence between the rapidly expanding video game industry and contemporary art. As first-person shooter (FPS) games such as *Doom* (1993), *Quake* (1996), and *Wolfenstein 3D* (1992) gained massive popularity, they captivated a generation of gamers while also attracting avant-garde artists seeking new forms of creative expression.

This period saw the emergence of art mods - modifications of commercial video games undertaken by artists for purposes that extend beyond traditional gameplay. Art mods challenge conventional boundaries of art and play by transforming games into interactive artworks. They use environments designed for entertainment to question institutional hierarchies, aesthetic conventions, and even the role of the player in digital culture.

The central question of this essay is: How did artists use FPS games as a medium for critical and artistic expression during the 1990s, and how were these works received?

Play, Creativity, and the Origins of Games

From the earliest days of digital culture, play and experimentation have been central to human creativity. Johan Huizinga, in *Homo Ludens: A Study of the Play Element in Culture* (1938), argued that play predates organized culture, serving as a foundational aspect of human experience. Play is inherently creative and identity-forming, yet it is structured by rules. Some individuals, however, are drawn to bending or breaking these rules—asking, *what if we do it differently? Could we invent our own rules entirely?* This curiosity and willingness to transgress established boundaries have historically fueled innovation and invention.

The birth of video games

In the 1960s, programmers at MIT, including Steve Russell, developed *Spacewar!* on a PDP-1 computer - a game that existed entirely outside the original military and scientific purposes of the machine. By transforming a computational tool into a platform for play, these pioneers demonstrated that creativity often arises from technical curiosity and rule-breaking. *Spacewar!* introduced core mechanics that would influence countless future games, such as real-time player control, physics-based movement, and competitive multiplayer gameplay.

During the 1970s, this spirit of experimentation moved into the arcade and home computing spaces. Games like *Pong* (1972, Atari) simplified digital interaction into competitive gameplay, while *Breakout* (1976) and *Adventure* (1979, Atari 2600) expanded on puzzle-solving, exploration, and narrative elements. Home computers such as the Apple II, Commodore PET, and TRS-80 allowed hobbyist programmers to experiment with their own designs, giving rise to early software creativity outside the professional industry.

The early 1980s saw a dramatic expansion in personal computer capabilities, enabling more complex gameplay and visual expression. Platforms such as the Commodore 64, Sinclair ZX Spectrum, and Atari 8-bit family offered more memory, color graphics, and sound channels, which hobbyist developers and small studios leveraged to produce games like *Manic Miner* (1983), *Elite* (1984), and *Jet*

Set Willy (1984). These titles not only explored platforming, open-world exploration, and procedural generation, but also encouraged users to experiment with modifying games or creating their own software inspired by them.

This trajectory—from *Spacewar!*'s experimental use of the PDP-1 to sophisticated home computer games—demonstrates how playful experimentation, technical curiosity, and community collaboration continually pushed digital systems toward new artistic and interactive possibilities, setting the stage for the modding and art-game movements of the 1990s.

The Demoscene

Parallel to commercial game development, the demoscene and early computer art culture emerged. Groups bypassed copy protections and added "cracktros" with original graphics, animation, and music, demonstrating the creative potential of technical manipulation.

Early artistic demos often combined impressive visual effects with original chiptune music, creating a new form of digital performance. On Commodore 64, groups such as *Fairlight* and *The Future Crew* gained fame for their intricate intros and demos that showcased scrolling text, 3D wireframe graphics, and synchronized soundtracks.

On the Atari ST and Amiga platforms, groups like *Spaceballs* and *Mosaic* experimented with color cycling, raster effects, and early forms of procedural animation. These demos were often distributed through disk magazines or bulletin board systems (BBS), reaching audiences that valued both technical ingenuity and artistic creativity. Even the infamous crack intros—initially designed to credit groups for removing copy protection—became a space for playful, experimental graphics, music, and narrative, blending art and hacking culture in ways that prefigured later digital art movements.

The demoscene's emphasis on pushing hardware to its limits and exploring new aesthetic possibilities laid the foundation for early game-based artistic experimentation. It cultivated a generation of creators who saw code itself as a medium, foreshadowing the later rise of art mods, interactive installations, and independent digital games.

The Rise of Game Modding

The early 1990s saw first-person shooter (FPS) games introducing sophisticated engines that allowed for extensive user modification. id Software, the developer behind *Doom* and *Quake*, actively encouraged player-driven content creation. Level editors and tools such as WAD (Where's All the Data) files enabled players to create custom maps, textures, and even modify game mechanics. Communities of amateur modders rapidly formed online, exchanging maps, mods, and creative hacks that ranged from humorous parodies to technical experiments.

For *Doom*, some of the most famous early mods included *Alien Vendetta* and *Final Doom*, which pushed level design and difficulty to extremes, while lighter, humorous mods like *Doom RPG* and *Chex Quest* repurposed the engine for comedic or promotional purposes. Creative experiments like *Brutal Doom* later added new weapons, gore effects, and physics tweaks, showing how mods could radically transform gameplay.

Similarly, *Quake* became a fertile ground for experimentation. Mods such as *Team Fortress*, originally a *Quake* mod before becoming its own franchise, introduced team-based multiplayer mechanics that reshaped the FPS genre. *Quake Army Knife* and *Quoth* showcased technical ingenuity, enabling new map styles, scripting features, and aesthetic effects. Other mods, like *Dissolution of Eternity*, explored surreal or narrative-driven experiences, emphasizing the engine's potential for artistic expression beyond traditional gameplay.

These early modding communities were crucial for both gaming culture and digital creativity. They demonstrated that players could act as co-creators, extending and transforming the original games in ways the developers themselves had not envisioned. This participatory model laid the foundation for later artistic experimentation, where the game engine itself became a medium for expression, ultimately inspiring the early generation of art mods.

Digital and Conceptual Art Influences

Parallel to developments in game modding, the 1980s and early 1990s witnessed the growth of digital and interactive art. In conceptual art, the deconstruction of traditional media and the questioning of institutional authority were already established practices.

Art mods emerged at the intersection of digital art, conceptual practice, and game culture. The late 1980s and early 1990s saw digital and interactive art gaining traction, with artists experimenting with virtual environments, interactivity, and algorithmic processes. Conceptual art traditions, emphasizing institutional critique and the deconstruction of established media, provided further intellectual grounding.

A parallel development occurred in net.art, an artistic practice that emerged in the mid-1990s focused on the Internet as a medium for experimentation and critique. Net.art artists interrogated the very structure, logic, and protocols of the network, often deconstructing its expected uses and highlighting its social, economic, and political dimensions. For example, Olia Lialina's *My Boyfriend Came Back from the War* (1996) used the browser as a narrative space, fragmenting linear storytelling and engaging the user in navigating nonlinear, interactive media. This approach shares a conceptual kinship with art mods: both repurpose existing digital infrastructures (game engines or web protocols) to produce works that are not intended by the original system designers.

Both art mods and net.art demonstrate creativity through technological transgression. Just as Jodi manipulated *Quake* to foreground the logic of the game engine, net.art deconstructs the browser, hyperlinks, and networked interactivity to reveal underlying structures and challenge conventional expectations. In this sense, the experimentation of net.art situates art mods within a broader lineage of digital practices that explore, subvert, and expand the potential of computational media.

Within this context, FPS games with modifiable engines offered an unprecedented opportunity. Games such as *Doom* and *Quake* allowed users to manipulate levels, textures, and mechanics, effectively turning the game engine into a creative medium. Just as the demoscene explored aesthetic expression through technical mastery, art mods leveraged the same possibilities to produce works that were simultaneously interactive, critical, and conceptually rigorous.

Early Art Mods

Several pioneering works from the mid-1990s illustrate the emergence of art mods as a distinct form of digital art.

ArsDoom (1995) – Orhan Kipcak and Team

One of the earliest known examples of an art mod is *ArsDoom* (1995), developed by Orhan Kipcak and his collaborators for presentation at Ars Electronica in Linz, Austria. Using the *Doom II* engine, the artists transformed the game into a virtual museum where the player could "shoot" at artworks and representations of artists themselves.

This work functioned as a critique of the contemporary art world, turning the violent conventions of FPS games into a metaphor for institutional critique. By appropriating a mass-market entertainment medium and inserting it into a high-art context, *ArsDoom* highlighted the performative and destructive potentials inherent in interactive digital spaces.

Museum Meltdown Series (1996–1999) – Palle Torsson & Tobias Bernstrup

Following *ArsDoom*, the Swedish artists Palle Torsson and Tobias Bernstrup created the *Museum Meltdown* series using the *Duke Nukem 3D* engine. Each iteration reconstructed actual museum spaces—such as Arken Museum in Denmark and Moderna Museet in Stockholm—allowing players to navigate and interact with digital replicas of cultural institutions.

However, the key artistic gesture was subversive: players could "destroy" the artworks and manipulate the museum space in ways impossible in reality. The series interrogated institutional authority, questioning the sanctity of the museum and the role of the spectator. It was simultaneously a humorous, playful intervention and a pointed critique of power dynamics in art spaces.

Jodi (Untitled Game, 1996–2001)

The Belgian-Dutch duo Jodi represents a conceptual turn in art modding. Their *Untitled Game* modifications of *Quake*, alongside earlier work such as *SOD* (a *Wolfenstein 3D* mod), deconstructed the conventions of gameplay entirely. Graphics were abstracted or glitched, levels were often non-navigable, and standard objectives were rendered meaningless.

Jodi's work emphasized the materiality and logic of the game engine itself, transforming it into an aesthetic object. Unlike the satirical destruction in *Museum Meltdown*, Jodi pursued an abstract, almost anti-game approach. Their work was exhibited at Documenta X (1997) and widely recognized in the net.art community, helping to establish art mods as a legitimate form of contemporary art practice.

First Museum Shooter

In the mid-to-late 1990s, a distinct subgenre of art mods emerged that has been referred to as "First Museum Shooters" - FPS-based art mods that explicitly situate gameplay within the architecture of art institutions. Unlike conventional first-person shooters, which emphasize combat and objectives, these mods transpose the mechanics of FPS games into museum or gallery environments, inviting players to engage critically with cultural spaces.

One of the earliest and most cited examples is *ArsDoom* (1995) by Orhan Kipcak and collaborators, which transformed the *Doom II* engine into a virtual museum. Visitors could navigate galleries, interact with artworks, and even "destroy" pieces, subverting the traditional roles of viewer and curator. Similarly, the *Museum Meltdown series* (1996–1999) by Palle Torsson and Tobias Bernstrup reconstructed real museum interiors—such as Moderna Museet in Stockholm—allowing players to explore, manipulate, and destabilize canonical art spaces. These mods convert the museum from a static, authoritative environment into a participatory, mutable space where the audience is both observer and actor.

A more recent continuation of this genre is *DOOM: The Gallery Experience* (2022), a fan-made mod that reimagines the classic *DOOM* engine as an art exhibition space. Instead of corridors filled with demons, players wander through galleries with a glass of wine in their hand, instead of a gun, looking at digital artworks, photography, and paintings from the Met Open Access Collection, rendered as textures on the walls. By appropriating one of the most iconic FPS engines, the project playfully blurs the line between gaming and curatorial practice, echoing the critical strategies of earlier works like *ArsDoom* and *Museum Meltdown*. It demonstrates that the fascination with transforming museums into playable, interactive arenas remains alive decades later, and that the FPS engine still serves as a potent medium for questioning how art is displayed, consumed, and experienced.

First Museum Shooters engage with player agency and interactivity in ways that traditional museum visits cannot. The FPS mechanics—movement, targeting, shooting—are repurposed to challenge social and cultural conventions rather than simulate violence alone. The visual and spatial fidelity of the museum interiors contrasts with the anarchic potential of player interaction: players can destroy or rearrange artworks, creating a tension between realism and chaos. This interplay mirrors broader conceptual art practices, where disruption of norms is itself a creative gesture. The games thus function not only as interactive critiques but as meta-artworks, reflecting on the relationship between space, authority, play, and creativity in contemporary culture.

Deconstruction of Gameplay

A defining strategy of many art mods is the deliberate deconstruction of gameplay, challenging the conventions of digital entertainment and prompting reflection on the medium itself. By altering or removing core mechanics, these works transform familiar game environments into spaces of conceptual and aesthetic inquiry.

One of the most notable examples is *Jodi* (Joan Heemskerk and Dirk Paesmans), whose mods for *Quake* and other FPS engines abstract graphics, strip away objectives, and disrupt standard user interfaces. In works like *SOD* (1995) and *Untitled Game* (1996–2001), players encounter fragmented textures, disorienting perspectives, and broken visual cues that render traditional gameplay impossible. These "unplayable" spaces foreground the materiality and logic of the game engine, forcing players to confront the underlying systems rather than merely completing in-game tasks. The glitch aesthetics—misaligned textures, distorted visuals, and erratic animations—serve simultaneously as technical critique and artistic expression, highlighting the medium's computational structures while questioning the assumptions of interactivity and user control.

From Hacking to Activism

In the early 2000s, art mods underwent a profound transformation. What initially began as playful experiments-hacking and modifying existing video games-evolved into powerful platforms for political activism and social commentary.

Online gaming and communities

At the turn of the millennium, FPS games were at the forefront of both gaming culture and online communities. Titles like *Quake III Arena* (1999), *Counter-Strike* (1999), *Battlefield 1942* (2002), and *Soldier of Fortune* (2000) replaced earlier classics such as *Doom* and *Quake*, offering fast-paced online multiplayer experiences. These games became central hubs for modding communities, providing artists and players with tools to experiment with game mechanics, environments, and aesthetics.

Velvet-Strike and the Turn Toward Political Art

As FPS technology advanced, art mods began to shift toward political engagement. A key example is *Velvet-Strike* (2002), created by Brody Condon, Joan Leandre, and Anne-Marie Schleiner. This project introduced digital graffiti sprays that could be deployed within *Counter-Strike*, transforming the militarized and often xenophobic game spaces into platforms for political intervention. Players could "tag" maps with anti-war and activist messages, challenging the game's dominant narratives and militaristic aesthetics. By integrating these artistic interventions into a popular online FPS, *Velvet-Strike* demonstrated the potential for games to function as sites of political expression rather than merely entertainment.

Joseph DeLappe: *dead-in-iraq*

Simultaneously, Joseph DeLappe emerged as a pioneer in politically driven activism in on-line games. In *dead-in-iraq* (2006–2011), he entered the U.S. Army's recruitment game *America's Army* and typed the names of soldiers killed in Iraq into the game's chat interface. This intervention transformed the game from a recruitment tool into a virtual memorial and critique, turning a space designed to simulate military action into a platform for reflection and remembrance.

DeLappe continued this trajectory with works such as *Elegy: GTA USA Gun Homicides*, a performance in *Grand Theft Auto V* overlaying real-world data on gun deaths onto the game world. Through these projects, DeLappe leveraged the immersive qualities of FPS games to confront players with uncomfortable social realities, illustrating how game environments can become arenas for political activism.

The evolution of art mods during the early 2000s reflects a broader trend in digital art: the medium of video games became a space for both aesthetic experimentation and political engagement. FPS games, with their immersive worlds and multiplayer connectivity, provided artists with the perfect arena to challenge conventional narratives and explore activism within virtual environments. Projects like *Velvet-Strike* and Joseph DeLappe's interventions demonstrate how art mods have transformed from playful technical experiments into platforms for meaningful social and political discourse.

A New Generation of Game Engines

By the late 1990s and around 2000, game engines such as *Unreal* and *Marathon Infinity* had become particularly attractive to artists working with art mods. These engines offered capabilities that differed significantly from earlier mod-friendly engines like *Doom* and *Quake*. While *Doom* and *Quake* allowed users to create custom levels, textures, and gameplay tweaks, they were primarily designed for fast-paced first-person shooting, with limited scripting options and relatively rigid game mechanics. *Unreal* and *Marathon Infinity*, in contrast, provided far greater flexibility in shaping the environment, designing interactive elements, and constructing narrative structures.

Unreal, through its level editor and scripting language *UnrealScript*, allowed artists to craft highly detailed environments and manipulate interactivity in ways that went beyond the simple triggers and weapon modifications possible in earlier engines. *Marathon Infinity*, though not as graphically advanced, supported complex scenario creation and narrative branching, giving artists the ability to experiment with storytelling and player experience in three-dimensional spaces.

This technical flexibility opened new possibilities for artistic expression. Where earlier mods often focused on retexturing, humorous interventions, or minor gameplay alterations, the newer engines enabled immersive and conceptually ambitious works. Artists could construct surreal architectures, manipulate spatial perception, or create interactive narratives that challenge conventional ideas of gameplay.

The exhibition: Synreal – The Unreal Modification

In 1999, the exhibition *Synreal – The Unreal Modification* was held at the Institute for New Culture Technologies (Institut für Neue Kulturtechnologien) in Vienna, marking a significant moment in the intersection of digital art and gaming culture. Curated by Konrad Becker, the exhibition featured a diverse array of artists who utilized the *Unreal Engine* to create innovative game modifications that blurred the lines between interactive entertainment and contemporary art.

The *Unreal Engine*, released in 1998, provided artists with a powerful platform for experimentation. Its advanced graphics capabilities, coupled with the inclusion of *UnrealEd*—the game's level editor—enabled creators to design immersive environments and interactive narratives. This accessibility allowed artists to manipulate the game's architecture, textures, and gameplay mechanics to convey conceptual ideas and artistic expressions.

Artists like Margarete Jahrmann and Max Moswitzer contributed to the exhibition with works that explored themes of identity and digital interaction. Jahrmann's piece, *superfem*, allowed players to engage with different operating system interfaces, reflecting on the fluidity of digital identities. Similarly, Moswitzer's work delved into the complexities of virtual spaces and user interaction within them.

Axel Stockburger's *Loopwalker* focused on the auditory experience within the Unreal Engine. By positioning 150 sound loops in various rooms, Stockburger created a spatial sound environment that challenged traditional notions of audio-visual interaction in digital spaces. The spherical room design and concentric sound arrangement invited players to experience sound as a dynamic element within the game world.

Synreal stands as a pioneering example of how game engines like Unreal can transcend their original purpose to become platforms for artistic expression. By embracing the tools and languages of digital gaming, artists were able to create works that not only entertained but also provoked thought and discussion about the evolving relationship between technology, identity, and art.

The popularity of *Unreal* and *Marathon Infinity* among artists can thus be understood as a response to both technical and conceptual opportunities. The engines' increased flexibility allowed artists to transcend the limitations of earlier modding platforms and engage in deeper explorations of space, narrative, and interaction. Art mods produced during this period were no longer simply playful experiments within existing commercial games; they became immersive, narrative-driven, and conceptually rich works that leveraged the medium's potential as a tool for artistic expression. This period represents a high point in the intersection of contemporary art and game modification, immediately preceding the broader shift toward independently developed art games, where artists would increasingly create their own engines or use simpler tools to realize their visions.

Reception of Art Mods

Art World Reception

Within the traditional art world, art mods have experienced a mix of acceptance and skepticism. Some curators and critics have recognized the innovative potential of art mods, showcasing them in prominent exhibitions. For instance, the *Velvet-Strike* mod was featured in the 2004 Whitney Biennial, highlighting its artistic merit and the growing intersection between digital culture and contemporary art. Similarly, Joseph DeLappe's *dead-in-iraq* project, which involved memorializing fallen soldiers in the game *America's Army*, has been presented in various art venues, emphasizing the political and performative aspects of gaming.

However, this recognition has not been universal. Many in the art world have viewed art mods as ephemeral or lacking the permanence associated with traditional art forms. The integration of video games into art exhibitions was sometimes seen as a novelty rather than a legitimate artistic endeavor. This skepticism was compounded by concerns over the commercial nature of video games and their association with entertainment rather than cultural critique.

Academic Reception

Academically, art mods have gradually gained attention, though not without initial resistance. Early scholars were hesitant to engage with video games, viewing them as popular culture artifacts unworthy of serious academic inquiry. This reluctance was rooted in a broader academic bias that privileged traditional forms of art and culture, often dismissing digital and interactive media as trivial or unserious.

Over time, however, the field of game studies has emerged, providing a platform for the critical examination of video games as cultural and artistic objects. Scholars have analyzed art mods as forms of cultural criticism and political commentary, exploring their potential to challenge mainstream narratives and engage audiences in new ways. For example, research has highlighted how projects like *Velvet-Strike* and *dead-in-iraq* use the gaming environment as a medium for protest and reflection, demonstrating the capacity of video games to serve as platforms for artistic expression.

Gaming Communities

Within gaming communities, art mods have often been met with resistance or misunderstanding. Many gamers view modifications as enhancements to gameplay, such as new levels or features, rather than as artistic expressions. When artists introduced mods that altered gameplay mechanics or incorporated political messages, they were sometimes seen as disrupting the core gaming experience.

The introduction of mods like *Velvet-Strike*, which allowed players to spray anti-war graffiti within the game *Counter-Strike*, faced backlash from parts of the gaming community. Critics argued that such interventions were inappropriate and detracted from the game's intended purpose. This reaction underscores the tension between artistic expression and the expectations of traditional gaming audiences.

Despite this, some gamers have recognized the potential of art mods to expand the medium itself. By challenging assumptions about gameplay, interactivity, and narrative, art mods encourage players to reconsider the social, political, and aesthetic dimensions of digital play. This interaction between the artist, the game, and the player creates a feedback loop that fosters engagement across cultural and disciplinary boundaries.

The end of an era

Afte 2010, the practice of art mods started to fade. One major factor was the increasing commercialization of the game industry. As games became more graphically sophisticated and profitable, studios implemented stricter copyright protections and closed ecosystems, limiting the creative freedom that earlier moddable engines like *Quake* or *Half-Life* had offered. The legal risks associated with modifying commercial games—potential copyright infringement or DMCA takedowns—made art mods less viable.

At the same time, the broader art world was shifting. Institutions favored digital works that could be exhibited and preserved without the technical complexity or niche appeal of mods. The audience for art mods remained small and primarily within gaming communities, while galleries and museums increasingly embraced web-based art, interactive installations, and later mobile or social-media-driven projects.

Faced with these constraints, artists began to move away from modifying existing commercial games and toward creating their own games. The rise of affordable, accessible tools—such as GameMaker, Unity, Flash, and later Twine—

enabled artists to develop independent games that were both conceptually rich and technically feasible. This shift gave birth to a generation of art and independent games that could be distributed freely or cheaply, bypassing the limitations of mainstream engines. Notable examples include *Passage* (Jason Rohrer, 2007), *Every Day the Same Dream* (Molleindustria, 2009), and *Braid* (Jonathan Blow, 2008), all of which explored narrative, temporality, and player choice in ways that commercial games rarely did.

In this context, art mods reached a conceptual dead end. While early mods offered provocative reinterpretations of existing game spaces, their expressive potential was increasingly constrained by legal, technical, and commercial pressures. By developing independent games, artists regained control over the medium, turning limitations into creative opportunities. The end of art mods was not the end of artistic engagement with games; rather, it marked a transition from appropriating commercial engines to creating original works in new, more accessible formats.

The Museum Under Fire: From ArsDoom to Climate Activism

The term *First Museum Shooters* describes a strand of artistic practice that emerged in the mid-1990s, when contemporary artists began using first-person shooter (FPS) games to recreate and reimagine museums. Rooted in the modding culture of DOOM (1993), these works transformed the video game engine—originally designed for fast-paced combat—into a platform for institutional critique. Instead of wandering virtual dungeons, players now navigated replicas of art galleries and cultural institutions, where the mechanics of aiming, firing, and destroying were turned against the very objects and spaces traditionally associated with preservation and reverence.

The origins of this phenomenon lie in a convergence of cultural forces. On one side, the video game industry of the early 1990s was rapidly developing new genres, with DOOM and other FPS titles establishing an aesthetic of immersion, agency, and violence that would define digital play for decades. Just as important, DOOM's mod-friendly design—its architecture of easily replaced maps and assets—invited players to build new worlds, giving rise to a participatory culture of level design, hacks, and machinima. On the other side, the art world was grappling with questions of authorship, authenticity, and the role of institutions. The 1990s saw a surge of practices often labelled "new media art" or "Game Art," where artists turned emerging technologies into tools for critical reflection.

It is in this intersection that *First Museum Shooters* arose. By placing museums inside FPS engines, artists exposed the tension between the museum's traditional role as a site of conservation and the FPS's default mechanics of destruction. They also highlighted generational and cultural shifts: from passive spectatorship toward participatory, often irreverent forms of engagement. In works such as *ArsDoom* (1995) and *Museum Meltdown* (1996–1999), the museum was not a sanctuary but a battleground, an arena where art could be shot, exploded, and remade. Later works like *Jeff Koons Must Die!!!* (2011) pushed the critique further, confronting not just institutions but also the cult of celebrity artists.

Seen in context, *First Museum Shooters* belong both to the history of video games—where modding and user-generated content democratized creative tools—and to the history of contemporary art, where destruction, parody, and institutional critique have long been strategies of resistance. These works show how the logic of the FPS, once confined to demon-filled dungeons, could be repurposed to question the very structures that define what art is, where it belongs, and who has the right to interact with it.

DOOM and the Birth of the First-Person Shooter

When DOOM was released by id Software in 1993, it marked a turning point not only in video game design but in digital culture as a whole. While not the first game to use a first-person perspective—earlier titles such as *Maze War* (1974) and *Wolfenstein 3D* (1992) had already experimented with the format—DOOM crystallized the genre and defined the mechanics, aesthetics, and cultural aura of what would become known as the first-person shooter (FPS).

At its core, DOOM presented players with a simple but revolutionary combination: fast-paced action viewed through the eyes of the protagonist, labyrinthine 3D environments rendered with real-time graphics, and an arsenal of weapons designed for both empowerment and excess. The player's body was reduced to a gun and a motion perspective, creating an experience that was immersive, visceral, and immediate.

Technical and Cultural Innovation

DOOM's impact was not only due to its gameplay but also to its technological innovations. Its pseudo-3D graphics engine, advanced for its time, allowed for fluid movement, dynamic lighting, and atmospheric level design. Multiplayer functionality, particularly the introduction of deathmatch, created a new social form of play that would become a cornerstone of competitive gaming.

Equally important was DOOM's open architecture. By separating the core engine from its data files (WADs), id Software enabled players to create their own levels, textures, and modifications. This decision seeded a thriving modding culture, where fans extended DOOM far beyond its original form—creating new maps, total conversions, and eventually influencing entire genres. In this sense, DOOM was both a game and a platform, democratizing game design at a moment when most development tools were inaccessible to the public.

Defining the FPS Genre

The influence of DOOM on the FPS genre is so profound that for much of the 1990s, FPS games were casually referred to as "DOOM clones." The formula of moving through corridors, shooting enemies, and collecting keys and weapons became a design template that countless titles imitated and refined. Games such as *Quake* (1996), *Half-Life* (1998), and *Halo: Combat Evolved* (2001) each built upon DOOM's foundation, adding full 3D environments, narrative depth, and refined multiplayer systems.

Beyond mechanics, DOOM also established the cultural identity of the FPS: the mix of speed, violence, and adrenaline-fueled action that resonated with players and critics alike. It shaped expectations for immersion, control responsiveness, and player agency, setting a standard against which future shooters would be judged.

The Legacy of DOOM

Three decades after its release, DOOM's legacy continues to shape gaming. Its code has been ported to almost every device imaginable, from ATMs to smartwatches, becoming an internet meme in its own right. The series itself has been periodically revived, most notably with *DOOM* (2016) and *DOOM Eternal* (2020), which reintroduced the franchise to a new generation while staying true to the original's emphasis on speed and combat rhythm.

Perhaps most significantly, DOOM demonstrated that games could evolve beyond closed entertainment products into cultural platforms—objects of creativity, community, and critique. The thriving modding culture around DOOM anticipated today's ecosystems of user-generated content in games like *Minecraft*, *Roblox*, and *Fortnite*. Its multiplayer innovations foreshadowed the rise of esports and online competitive play. And its blend of violence and interactivity continues to inspire debates about the social and cultural meaning of video games.

ArsDoom: The First Museum Shooter (1995)

The origins of the First Museum Shooter can be traced back to 1995, when Austrian media artist Orhan Kipcak created *ArsDoom* for the Ars Electronica festival in Linz, Austria. Built on the engine of DOOM II, the project is widely considered the very first example of a museum transposed into a first-person shooter.

Kipcak reconstructed the Brucknerhaus, the main exhibition hall of Ars Electronica, as a playable level. Instead of demons and hellscapes, the environment contained virtual replicas of the festival's artworks, installations, and even avatars of the exhibiting artists themselves. Visitors could walk through the digital museum, but rather than quietly viewing the works, they were given the familiar DOOM arsenal of guns and explosives. This meant that the art on display could be shot, destroyed, or obliterated at will. In a further twist, players could also "kill" the exhibiting artists, reducing them to the same status as enemies in a video game.

The decision to build *ArsDoom* was both practical and conceptual. On the practical level, DOOM was an accessible, moddable platform, widely recognized and easy to adapt. On the conceptual level, Kipcak used the game's violent mechanics to comment on the cultural and generational gap between the traditions of the art world and the emerging culture of digital play. By reimagining the gallery as a space of combat, *ArsDoom* highlighted the contradictions between a museum's role in preservation and the destructive possibilities offered by digital simulation.

For visitors, the experience was provocative and unsettling. To enter a museum is normally to adopt a position of reverence and restraint: one looks but does not touch. *ArsDoom* inverted this contract, inviting participants to actively dismantle the very art they had come to see. In doing so, it raised fundamental questions: What does it mean to destroy art in a digital copy? Is this vandalism, critique, or simply play?

In retrospect, *ArsDoom* established the template for later First Museum Shooters such as *Museum Meltdown* and *Jeff Koons Must Die!!!*. It demonstrated that video games could serve as powerful tools of institutional critique, turning the mechanics of popular culture against the structures of high culture. As the first work to transform a real exhibition space into an FPS arena, *ArsDoom* opened a new chapter in the dialogue between art and video games.

Museum Meltdown: The Museum Under Siege (1996-99)

If *ArsDoom* was the spark, then *Museum Meltdown* was the full ignition of the First Museum Shooter as an artistic strategy. Between 1996 and 1999, Swedish artists Palle Torsson and Tobias Bernstrup developed a series of works under this title, using the engines of popular FPS games to reconstruct real museums as playable battlefields.

The project began in 1996 at the ARKEN Museum of Modern Art in Copenhagen, where Torsson and Bernstrup used the *Duke Nukem 3D* engine to build a faithful 3D model of the institution. Visitors could walk through the familiar galleries, but instead of encountering quiet contemplation, they found hostile enemies, weapons, and the possibility of unleashing violence upon both artworks and architecture.

The concept evolved further in subsequent iterations: in 1997, *Museum Meltdown II* recreated the Contemporary Art Centre (CAC) in Vilnius, and by 1999, the artists had ported the project into the more advanced *Half-Life* engine for a reconstruction of Stockholm's Moderna Museet. Each new version expanded the technical fidelity, making the museums more realistic and the contrast between their real-world function—preservation and reverence—and their virtual transformation into war zones even more stark.

The artistic intention was clear. *Museum Meltdown* turned the museum itself into a paradoxical space: the very institution designed to protect and conserve cultural treasures was reimagined as a site of chaos, destruction, and combat. The player, cast in the role of the traditional FPS hero, was given freedom to navigate and to violate the sanctity of the institution. For some, this was cathartic and thrilling; for others, it was disturbing, as the game mechanics highlighted how fragile cultural spaces could appear when translated into interactive form.

Torsson and Bernstrup's work also tapped into broader debates in the 1990s about the authority of cultural institutions. Just as younger generations were embracing video games as a primary cultural form, museums still clung to hierarchical, object-focused traditions. By placing the museum inside a game engine best known for explosions and alien battles, the artists staged a generational clash: the seriousness of high art versus the irreverence of gaming culture.

Museum Meltdown quickly gained recognition as one of the most important works of early Game Art. It built directly on the pioneering step of *ArsDoom*, but took the idea further by choosing not a temporary festival exhibition, but established, prestigious art institutions as its setting. In doing so, it sharpened the critique: these were not just playful experiments, but direct confrontations with the authority of the museum itself.

In retrospect, *Museum Meltdown* stands as a landmark in the history of art and games. It not only demonstrated how FPS mechanics could be used for institutional critique, but like its predecessor, *Museum Meltdown* asked audiences to question what a museum is, who it serves, and what happens when the rules of interaction are rewritten by digital play.

Quake Hamburger Kunsthalle Reconstruction (1999)

In 1999, German artists Florian Muser and Imre Oswald brought the First Museum Shooter into the context of the Hamburger Kunsthalle. Using the engine of *Quake*, they meticulously rebuilt the architecture of the Kunsthalle's galleries, transforming one of Germany's most prestigious museums into an FPS arena. Visitors entering the virtual museum encountered not hushed corridors but a space populated by monsters and weapons, encouraging the player to navigate and battle through rooms that, in reality, were reserved for contemplation.

As with earlier works like *Museum Meltdown*, the juxtaposition between preservation and destruction was at the heart of the project. The Kunsthalle, a symbol of cultural continuity and authority, became a stage for chaos. By choosing *Quake*—a title notorious for its dark, gothic aesthetic and frenetic combat—the artists emphasized the tension between institutional order and the FPS's anarchic play. The work highlighted not only the fragility of cultural spaces in a digital context but also the ways in which virtual architecture could be appropriated for critique.

Stephen Honegger & Anthony Hunt's Container (2002)

The Australian artists Stephen Honegger and Anthony Hunt contributed to the lineage of the First Museum Shooter with their work *Container* (2002), first exhibited at Gertrude Contemporary Art Space in Melbourne. At first glance, the installation presented visitors with a puzzling sight: inside the gallery stood a full-scale shipping container. The absurdity of the situation immediately provoked a question—how could such an enormous object possibly have been maneuvered through the narrow doors and corridors of the art space? The answer lay, paradoxically, inside the container itself.

Within the container, visitors found a video projection. The film was a machinima, produced using the game engine of *Half-Life*, one of the most influential first-person shooters of the late 1990s. The video depicted a mysterious intruder breaking into the Gertrude Contemporary building by climbing through a back window. The figure navigated the institution's corridors and staircases in the manner of a typical FPS protagonist, before reaching the gallery space. There, he discovered a hidden hatch in the wall, pressed a button, and triggered a fantastical sequence: the gallery's roof opened up and a massive container was slowly lowered into the exhibition space.

The machinima concluded on a darkly ironic note. The intruder armed himself with a gun, approached the container, opened its door, and found a lone man watching a video inside. Without hesitation, he shot the man—closing the narrative loop between the player's destructive agency in an FPS and the passive role of a museum visitor in front of an artwork.

In linking machinima to installation practice, the artists bridged two worlds: the physical presence of the shipping container and the digital narrative explaining its arrival. The climactic moment, in which the intruder kills the video-watching figure, underscored the collapse of boundaries between observer and participant, art and play, fiction and reality. Here the FPS language of violence was not merely a tool for parody, but a structural device to question spectatorship itself.

Within the genealogy of First Museum Shooters, *Container* stands out as a conceptual inversion. Rather than reconstructing a museum within a game engine, as in *ArsDoom* or *Museum Meltdown*, it imported the logic of the FPS into the gallery, weaving together installation, machinima, and game aesthetics. In doing so, Honegger and Hunt expanded the genre's vocabulary, showing how the destructive play of video games could be reimagined not only as institutional critique but also as a meditation on the porousness between real and virtual cultural spaces.

Chris Reilly's SAIC Half-Life 2 Project (2006)

In 2006, for the graduate thesis exhibition at the School of the Art Institute of Chicago (SAIC), American artist Chris Reilly undertook an ambitious project: a full-scale reconstruction of the entire exhibition space, encompassing roughly 4,500 square feet across three floors, within the engine of *Half-Life 2*. The resulting work carried the lengthy title:

Everything I Do Is Art, But Nothing I Do Makes Any Difference, Part II: Or: How I Learned to Stop Worrying and Love the Gallery

The title itself was a clear allusion to Stanley Kubrick's 1964 film *Dr. Strangelove or: How I Learned to Stop Worrying and Love the Bomb*, highlighting a sensibility of dark humor and ironic critique that pervades the work. Just as Kubrick's film juxtaposed absurdity and existential threat, Reilly's installation juxtaposed the familiar rituals of gallery spectatorship with the unpredictable violence and agency of a first-person shooter.

Visitors to the SAIC exhibition had a dual experience. They could walk through the physical gallery, observing student artworks in situ, or enter the virtual reconstruction, navigating the same space digitally. In the virtual version, however, the rules of engagement were dramatically altered. Players encountered monsters, obstacles, and the possibility of destroying the artworks themselves—a direct invocation of the conventions established by earlier First Museum Shooters such as *ArsDoom* and *Museum Meltdown*.

Reilly added an inventive feature that distinguished his work: the ability to pick up paint cans scattered throughout the building and "shoot" them at walls and objects. When fired, the paint exploded, spreading in vibrant formations across surfaces—a digital echo of Niki de Saint Phalle's *Shooting Paintings* (1961–1962). In her performances, Saint Phalle fired a salon rifle at paint-filled containers mounted on reliefs and sculptures, allowing the resulting splatters to transform the objects into dynamic compositions. For Saint Phalle, this gesture was both a claim to agency in a male-dominated art world and a radical rethinking of painting as a process-oriented, participatory practice.

By integrating this mechanic, Reilly not only paid homage to Saint Phalle but also updated her concept for the language of digital interactivity. In his virtual gallery, the visitor could literally perform a "shooting painting," blending critique, play, and creation. The work thus interrogated the boundaries between observer and participant, destruction and authorship, physical and digital art, and reflected on the evolving role of the museum in the era of video games.

In *Everything I Do Is Art...*, Reilly extended the vocabulary of First Museum Shooters: where earlier works focused on institutional critique through destruction, he added a layer of performative creation, emphasizing both the agency of the player and the malleability of the exhibition as a cultural space. The piece demonstrated that FPS mechanics could be harnessed not only to challenge authority but also to expand the possibilities of artistic engagement itself.

Paul Steen's Art Assault (2010)

Swedish artist Paul Steen contributed to the evolution of First Museum Shooters with his project *Art Assault*, a modification of the free, open-source first-person shooter *AssaultCube*. Unlike previous works that reconstructed specific museums or galleries, Steen's project combined procedural gameplay, real-world art references, and social commentary within the framework of a competitive FPS.

In *Art Assault*, the computer-controlled bots were named after the 100 most successful contemporary artists, according to artfacts.net. Players entered the game world in Team Deathmatch mode, where both human and AI participants were randomly divided into two opposing teams: Inside and Outside. The maps themselves were modeled on real-life artist-run galleries and alternative museums, grounding the game in actual cultural spaces while maintaining the chaotic logic of an FPS environment.

The work transformed the standard conventions of competitive gaming into a platform for art criticism. By giving players the opportunity to "attack" digital representations of galleries and artist figures, Steen highlighted the interplay between fame, institutional power, and the ritualized behaviors of both the art world and gaming culture. Each match became a miniature allegory for art-world hierarchies: the most prominent figures were present as avatars, yet vulnerable to the mechanics of play, reflecting the fragility of cultural status when translated into a participatory, gamified space.

Art Assault extended the lineage of First Museum Shooters by merging interactivity, digital reconstruction, and social commentary. Where earlier projects like *ArsDoom* and *Museum Meltdown* emphasized the destruction of physical or virtual galleries, Steen's work introduced a layer of systemic critique, where the rules of the game itself—teams, objectives, and AI behaviors—represented commentary on the institutional and reputational dynamics of the contemporary art world. In doing so, *Art Assault* demonstrated how FPS mechanics could not only subvert museums but also interrogate the networks of artists, institutions, and audiences that define cultural value.

Michiel van der Zanden's Pwned Paintings #2 (2008)

In 2008, Dutch artist Michiel van der Zanden created the machinima *Pwned Paintings #2*, a work that extends the language of the First Museum Shooter into a third-person perspective, rather than the first-person viewpoint more commonly associated with DOOM and *Half-Life* modifications. Drawing inspiration from action games like *Max Payne*, the piece follows a lone character navigating an art-historic collection, armed with a rifle, as they move through the galleries and shoot at the paintings, causing them to fall from the walls.

The title itself, *Pwned Paintings*, references a popular expression in gaming culture, particularly in competitive titles like *Counter-Strike*. To say "You just got pwned!" is to declare one's domination over an opponent, a combination of humiliation and victory. Van der Zanden's machinima applies this logic to the art world: the falling paintings become a metaphorical statement of defeat, a symbolic conquest of traditional institutions and established hierarchies.

The work functions as a generational manifesto. By literally knocking historic artworks from their pedestals, van der Zanden dramatizes the arrival of a new cohort of artists, asserting their right to participate in and reshape the cultural narrative. Just as previous generations of artists challenged established conventions—whether through avant-garde interventions, conceptual experiments, or performative acts—*Pwned Paintings #2* stages a digital rebellion. The gallery, once a space of reverence and preservation, becomes a dynamic battlefield where legacy and authority are temporarily suspended.

Technically, the machinima leverages the affordances of video game engines to simulate interactive destruction, translating the aesthetics and vocabulary of FPS and action games into an artistic critique. By adopting a third-person perspective, the work emphasizes the performativity of the act: the viewer observes the protagonist as both agent and performer, reinforcing the theatrical and symbolic dimensions of the destruction.

Pwned Paintings #2 thus extends the conceptual framework established by earlier First Museum Shooter works, such as *Museum Meltdown* and *ArsDoom*, while also differentiating itself through genre hybridity and generational commentary. Van der Zanden's machinima interrogates the power structures of the art world, celebrates the agency of the new artist, and demonstrates how videogame mechanics can be repurposed as a tool for both critique and cultural assertion. It is a vivid example of how the interactive and performative languages of gaming can be harnessed to comment on institutional authority, historical canon, and the ongoing evolution of artistic practice.

Jeff Koons Must Die!!! (2011)

By 2011, the First Museum Shooter had moved beyond the reconstruction of institutional spaces to take aim at the figures who dominated them. American artist Hunter Jonakin's *Jeff Koons Must Die!!!*, built in the *Unreal Tournament 3* engine and presented as a custom-built arcade cabinet, placed the player in a virtual gallery filled entirely with replicas of Jeff Koons' most famous works: *Balloon Dog*, *Michael Jackson and Bubbles*, *Puppy*, and others.

Armed with rocket launchers and machine guns, players could gleefully destroy these high-value icons of contemporary art. The game was more than catharsis: it staged a biting critique of Koons' celebrity status, the commodification of art, and the seemingly untouchable aura of certain cultural figures. By placing Koons' sculptures into a format defined by violence and destruction, Jonakin questioned whether the aura of the "masterpiece" could survive in an age of digital reproduction and interactivity.

The arcade cabinet format further underscored the clash between high and low culture: Koons, often criticized for elevating kitsch into multimillion-dollar luxury, was here reduced to fragile polygons within a coin-operated machine. *Jeff Koons Must Die!!!* thus extended the lineage of First Museum Shooters by targeting not just institutions but also the individuals who embodied the art world's power structures.

The Tradition of Destroying Art: From Performance to Protest

The act of destroying or violently intervening in artworks has a long and complex history, spanning avant-garde experimentation, individual protest, and politically motivated activism. Far from being merely destructive, these gestures often function as a form of critique—challenging institutions, questioning authorship, or confronting social norms.

One early and striking example comes from Mary Richardson, a suffragette who, in 1914, slashed Velázquez's *Rokeby Venus* at the National Gallery in London. Richardson's attack was a direct political statement: the violence against a revered artwork symbolized the denial of women's rights and agency in public life. Similarly, in 1974, Tony Shafrazi spray-painted "KILL LIES ALL" on Picasso's *Guernica* at the Museum of Modern Art in New York, using destruction as a means to comment on the political climate and the role of art in social discourse.

In the context of contemporary art, Niki de Saint Phalle transformed destruction into creation with her *Shooting Paintings* (1961–1962). In these performances, she fired a rifle at paint-filled containers mounted on reliefs and sculptures, letting the explosions of color cover the surfaces. For Saint Phalle, the act was twofold: a critique of a male-dominated art world and a radical rethinking of painting as a performative, participatory medium. Destruction was not the end of art, but a method of making art anew.

The act of destroying or radically altering art has long been a strategy for critique, protest, or performative exploration. Gustav Metzger, a pioneer of auto-destructive art, created works in the 1960s that were designed to physically erode, corrode, or burn over time, emphasizing impermanence and the fragility of cultural objects. In a different vein, British artist Michael Landy's 2001 performance *Break Down* involved systematically destroying all of his personal possessions—including artworks—within a former department store in London, transforming total annihilation into a conceptual reflection on value, materiality, and artistic identity.

More recently, Banksy has used destruction as a tool of subversion and commentary. His partially shredded *Girl With Balloon* (2018) and other site-specific interventions challenge the aura and commodification of artworks, turning moments of destruction into new forms of creation and public spectacle.

The tradition continued with digital and interactive works, such as the First Museum Shooters explored in this essay. In *ArsDoom*, *Museum Meltdown*, and *Jeff Koons Must Die!!!*, players replicate acts of destruction within virtual museums or galleries, subverting the authority of institutions and the sanctity of the art object through game mechanics. Here, destruction is simulated, yet the critique is tangible: the works question cultural hierarchies, commodification, and the untouchable aura of both artworks and artists.

This lineage of destructive gesture finds a contemporary echo in the actions of climate activists, such as the members of *Just Stop Oil*. In recent years, protestors have thrown soup, paint, or other substances onto famous masterpieces, including works by Van Gogh, Turner, and Banksy. While the artworks are often protected by glass or otherwise unharmed, the dramatic gestures generate widespread media attention and provoke public debate. The symbolic violence mirrors historical acts of art intervention: it disrupts the museum's authority, challenges cultural complacency, and creates a visible stage for urgent political messages.

The common thread linking these historical and contemporary practices is the use of destruction as a form of communication. Whether through the performative explosions of Saint Phalle, the digital annihilation in First Museum Shooters, or climate activists' theatrical attacks, these acts foreground the power and fragility of cultural objects, the contested nature of institutional authority, and the performativity inherent in the act of viewing and interacting with art. In today's context, where climate change presents an existential threat, these gestures of disruption are framed not as vandalism for its own sake, but as urgent, symbolic interventions that demand attention and provoke reflection.

The Continued Relevance of DOOM Modding in Museums and Contemporary Art

Even decades after its original release, *DOOM* remains a vibrant platform for creative experimentation, bridging videogame culture, art, and institutional critique. Its enduring relevance lies in the game's open architecture: the separation of engine and level files (WADs) allows artists, designers, and institutions to remix, reconstruct, and reimagine spaces within the familiar mechanics of a first-person shooter.

A striking contemporary example comes from the National Videogame Museum (NVM) in Frisco, Texas, which in recent years commissioned *NVM Doom*, a near 1:1 recreation of the museum inside the *DOOM II* engine. Visitors navigating the mod can explore the galleries, exhibition spaces, and stairwells of the museum as a playable level. The WAD even includes a "Tourist mode," removing enemies entirely, so users can wander leisurely through the environment, echoing the contemplative experience of an in-person museum visit. This project demonstrates how *DOOM* modding has evolved from informal fan bricolage into a professional, commissioned form of cultural mediation, where the museum itself becomes the subject and geometry of its own digital exhibition.

The flexibility of *DOOM* also supports more experimental and playful interventions. In early 2025, *DOOM: The Gallery Experience*—a meme-infused, interactive adaptation of galleries within the game engine—highlighted the continuing crossover between popular culture, gaming humor, and art critique. Such projects maintain the core logic of the First Museum Shooter: they transpose cultural spaces into a medium defined by interactivity, agency, and even simulated destruction, allowing audiences to inhabit, traverse, and question institutional spaces in novel ways.

Beyond museums, contemporary artists continue to use *DOOM* as a tool for artistic exploration and critique. By remapping real or imagined galleries into playable spaces, they challenge ideas of preservation, authority, and spectatorship. The act of modding *DOOM* becomes a performative gesture, emphasizing that digital spaces are malleable and participatory, and that art—like play—can be interrogated, reconfigured, and even "destroyed" to generate new meaning.

These recent examples underscore that *DOOM* modding is far from a historical curiosity. It remains a living practice, capable of mediating the relationship between games, art, and museums in ways that are both critically engaged and widely accessible. From the professional commissions of *NVM Doom* to meme-driven gallery experiments, *DOOM* continues to serve as a platform for reflection, creativity, and institutional critique, proving that the first-person shooter genre can be more than entertainment: it can be a lens through which we examine cultural spaces, histories, and practices.

Conclusion

The history of First Museum Shooters—from *ArsDoom* to *Jeff Koons Must Die!!!*—reveals a unique intersection between gaming, art, and institutional critique. By repurposing the violent mechanics of FPS games, artists have explored questions of authorship, authority, spectatorship, and cultural value, transforming museums into arenas of both playful engagement and pointed commentary. This lineage of digital destruction aligns with historical and contemporary acts of artistic intervention, from Saint Phalle's *Shooting Paintings* to the actions of climate activists, demonstrating that destruction can be a potent tool for reflection, critique, and social engagement.

Moreover, the continued relevance of *DOOM* modding in contemporary art and museum practice underscores the enduring potential of video games as platforms for experimentation, creativity, and institutional critique. Whether in commissioned projects, independent machinima, or playful meme-driven adaptations, First Museum Shooters remind us that cultural spaces are never fixed: they are interactive, malleable, and open to reimagination. The museum, once a sanctuary of preservation, can also be a battleground—a site where art is not only viewed but questioned, challenged, and reinvented through the language of play.

Playing with Failure: Glitch, Deconstruction, and Art in Video Games

When artists in the late 1990s and early 2000s began engaging seriously with videogames, many did not approach the medium as designers of new fantastical worlds. Instead, they chose to interrogate and dismantle existing ones. This act of deconstruction—stripping away the familiar illusion of realism to reveal code, rules, and hidden ideology—connected game-based practices to a much longer art-historical lineage: the sabotage of Dada, the rule-based instructions of Fluxus, the conceptual turn toward ideas over objects, and the postmodern suspicion of stable truths.

The philosophical backdrop for this impulse was shaped in large part by Jacques Derrida's theory of deconstruction, which profoundly influenced the art world from the 1970s onward. Derrida argued that texts, images, and systems are never self-contained or transparent but always rest upon contradictions, exclusions, and unspoken assumptions. Artists across disciplines—from literature and architecture to performance and visual art—translated this into a strategy of questioning representation itself. Instead of producing seamless illusions, they emphasized gaps, failures, and internal conflicts. By the turn of the millennium, videogames became a fertile ground for such exploration. What began as *art mods* and interventions in commercial game engines soon expanded into the broader field of glitch art, where digital error is revalued as both method and message.

Postmodern Deconstruction as Method

In Derrida's sense, deconstruction is not destruction but a critical practice: a way of reading that brings to light the hidden scaffolding of meaning. Within the arts this was translated into techniques of appropriation, fragmentation, and interruption—methods designed to prevent cultural forms from appearing "natural" or self-evident.

In game art, this meant shifting attention away from immersive storylines and towards the underlying apparatus of play: rendering pipelines, input loops, physics engines, and the cultural scripts embedded in genre conventions. Artists would deliberately slow these processes down, break them, or reroute them, forcing players to confront the machinery itself. The "text" to be read was no longer just the game's plot or imagery, but what Ian Bogost later called its procedural rhetoric—the arguments a system makes through its rules.

Thus, to deconstruct a game was to reveal how its pleasures and logics were constructed, and to challenge the authority of software by turning its hidden rules into visible, sometimes chaotic material.

In the late 1990s and early 2000s, a group of artists began treating commercial videogames not merely as entertainment but as systems to interrogate, dismantle, and reimagine. By exposing the underlying rules, code, and procedural logic of games, these artists questioned the assumptions embedded in digital play and highlighted the often invisible cultural and technical scaffolding of interactive worlds. Among the pioneers of this approach were JODI, Joan Leandre, Cory Arcangel, and Vuk Ćosić, each of whom used distinct strategies to deconstruct well-known games.

JODI *Untitled Game* (1996–2001)

JODI (Joan Heemskerk and Dirk Paesmans) was one of the earliest and most influential artists in this field. In *Untitled Game* (1996–2001), JODI used the *Quake* engine, exploiting map editors, asset tools, and QuakeC scripting to radically transform the familiar first-person shooter environment. Levels collapse into abstract geometries, textures dissolve into raw bitmaps, and HUDs misreport or vanish entirely. Conventional objectives and gameplay logic are disrupted, leaving players acutely aware of the procedural scaffolding that normally remains hidden. JODI continued this strategy in *SOD* (1999), a deconstruction of *Wolfenstein 3D*, where recognizable Nazi corridors are replaced with optical noise, ASCII-like textures, and jagged abstract planes, transforming the shooter into a kind of op-art labyrinth.

Joan Leandre *Retroyou* series (1999–2003)

Joan Leandre extended these deconstructive strategies into flight and racing simulators with his *Retroyou* series (1999–2003). By altering asset tables, physics parameters, and terrain streaming, Leandre produced surreal, glitch-like landscapes in which roads, skies, and buildings collapsed into fragmented, often navigable compression artifacts. Conventional objectives, such as winning races or completing missions, were abandoned, replaced by poetic drifts through corrupted simulation, emphasizing the underlying systems of code and logic rather than player skill.

Cory Arcangel *Super Mario Clouds* (2002

Cory Arcangel approached deconstruction through minimalism and abstraction. In *Super Mario Clouds* (2002), Arcangel removed nearly all elements from the original *Super Mario Bros.* ROM, leaving only drifting clouds against a blank sky. The platforming mechanics and narrative vanish, leaving the player to confront the game as a formal system rather than a site of entertainment. Cory Arcangel's *Space Invader* (2004) is a seminal example of deconstructive game art that manipulates the foundational mechanics of a classic video game to create a new, conceptually rich experience. In this work, Arcangel collaborated with Alex Galloway of the Radical Software Group to modify the Atari 2600 game *Space Invaders*. The modification involves erasing all but one of the alien invaders, resulting in a game that is nearly impossible to play. The sole remaining invader inherits the firing capabilities of all the others, leading to a rapid barrage of bullets that overwhelms the player within approximately one minute of gameplay .

Vuk Ćosić *The ASCII Unreal* (1999)

Vuk Ćosić further expanded deconstructive practices with a focus on text-based and code interventions. In *The ASCII Unreal* (1999), Ćosić converted the first-person shooter *Unreal Tournament* into a purely ASCII-rendered environment, replacing high-resolution textures with letters, numbers, and symbols. Gameplay mechanics remained functional, but the visual abstraction forced players to interpret the world differently, exposing the symbolic and procedural nature of digital environments. The work highlights how even hyper-realistic games are constructed from underlying systems of representation and logic, and it anticipates the later development of glitch art, where errors and unexpected behaviors are embraced as aesthetic and conceptual tools.

The History and Concept of Glitch Art

Glitch art is a contemporary art practice that foregrounds digital errors, malfunctions, and failures as aesthetic material. At its core, glitch art is an exploration of imperfection: it transforms technological failures—such as corrupted files, software bugs, or distorted audiovisual signals—into a creative strategy. By embracing the unexpected and uncontrollable, glitch artists challenge the smooth illusions of digital media, exposing the underlying systems and vulnerabilities of technology.

The origins of glitch art can be traced back to the late 1950s and 1960s, with early experiments in "error-based" visual art. Nam June Paik, often considered the father of video art, manipulated television signals to produce distorted images, creating works such as *TV Buddha* (1974) and signal interference pieces that anticipated the aesthetics of glitches decades later.

The term "glitch" itself originates in electronics and computing, referring to unexpected errors in circuits, software, or digital transmission. By the 1990s, as computers and digital media became widespread, a new generation of artists began deliberately exploiting software errors. This was a period closely aligned with the rise of art mods and deconstructive game art, where artists were manipulating commercial games to reveal their underlying mechanics. Both approaches share a fascination with the hidden rules and structures of digital systems, whether through corrupted code, distorted graphics, or altered game logic.

Rosa Menkman Glitch Moment(um) (2011)

Rosa Menkman is a Dutch artist and theorist renowned for her exploration of glitch aesthetics and the critical potential of digital errors. Her seminal work, *The Collapse of PAL* (2011), delves into the obsolescence of the PAL video standard, using analog feedback, compression artifacts, and digital manipulation to create a haunting audiovisual performance that mourns the loss of this analogue broadcasting system.

Central to Menkman's theoretical framework is the concept of the "glitch moment," a term she articulates in her publication *Glitch Moment(um)* (2011). She describes the glitch as an interruption that shifts an object away from its ordinary form and discourse, offering a momentary rupture that challenges conventional perceptions . This perspective aligns with her broader critique of digital media, where she examines how technological failures can reveal the underlying structures and ideologies embedded within digital systems.

Connection to Deconstructive Game Art and Art Mods

Glitch art and deconstructive game art intersect in their shared interest in revealing the underlying machinery of digital systems. Both practices challenge the polished veneer of software, whether by corrupting files, altering code, or remixing game engines. Early art mods, such as those by JODI, Joan Leandre, and Cory Arcangel, intentionally destabilized commercial games, exposing their procedural rhetoric and embedded cultural assumptions. Similarly, glitch art exploits technical errors to question assumptions about digital media's reliability, perfection, and neutrality.

In both cases, the artist's role shifts from creating a polished product to orchestrating a process of discovery, error, and revelation. The glitch—or the destabilized game world—becomes both medium and message, inviting audiences to reconsider the systems they take for granted, whether those systems are gameplay mechanics, software code, or networked digital environments.

From Streets to Screens: Performance Art and Online Worlds

Performance art emerged in the mid-1960s as a radical way to push the boundaries between art and everyday life. Building on earlier avant-garde experiments such as Dada and Futurism, artists in the 1960s and 70s sought to create works that could not be commodified, owned, or easily exhibited in museums. The movement was strongly influenced by Allan Kaprow's "Happenings," which emphasized participation, improvisation, and the blurring of art and life. Fluxus artists such as Yoko Ono and Nam June Paik likewise embraced ephemeral events, often minimal in form but socially provocative in effect.

Performance artists deliberately worked outside the established art system of galleries, curators, and collectors. Instead, performances often took place in public spaces—on the street, in squares, in abandoned buildings—where audiences encountered them unexpectedly. As RoseLee Goldberg has argued, performance was conceived as an antithesis to theatre: the goal was not illusion, narrative, or repetition but instead to create an ephemeral and authentic experience for performer and audience in an event that could not be repeated, captured or purchased.

Body and risk became central themes. Vito Acconci followed strangers on the streets of New York ("Following Piece," 1969); Chris Burden arranged to be shot in the arm by a friend ("Shoot," 1971); Marina Abramović and Ulay tested endurance and intimacy in works like "Rest Energy" (1980). Joseph Beuys famously declared "everyone is an artist," and staged politically charged performances that blurred symbolic ritual and social sculpture. These works confronted audiences with vulnerability, danger, sexuality, and social norms in ways that were immediate and often unsettling.

Given this history, it is not surprising that performance artists in the digital age have turned to computer games and online worlds. Just as earlier artists sought to bypass the white cube, today's artists use networked technologies to bypass geography altogether—bringing their art directly into people's living rooms. The internet enables global publics to witness, share, and even participate in live performances. Where 1960s artists occupied streets and squares, contemporary online performance artists occupy chatrooms, game servers, and 3D virtual platforms.

Antoinette LaFarge and the Plaintext Players

One of the earliest experiments in online performance was staged by Antoinette LaFarge, an American new media artist and professor at UC Irvine. In 1994, she founded the Plaintext Players, a troupe inspired by the text-based virtual environments known as MOOs (Multi-User Domains, Object-Oriented). These were descendants of the earlier MUDs, text-only spaces for roleplay and storytelling.

LaFarge describes her initial attraction to these platforms as a fascination with the space as between performing and being, and between writing and doing. The Players' first performance, *Christmas* (1994), unfolded across months in the PMC MOO, featuring archetypal characters—Big Man, Little Man, and Bloody Zelda—enacting surreal scenarios from courtroom dramas to desert wanderings. Like Kaprow's Happenings, these works were partially scripted but relied heavily on improvisation and chance encounters with online participants.

Joseph DeLappe: Nonviolence, Memory, and Digital Activism

The American artist Joseph DeLappe is one of the most prominent figures to have explored how virtual worlds can function as new arenas for art and political commentary. While his early interventions like *Howl* (2001) and *Dead-in-Iraq* (2006–2011) sought to disrupt the flow of online shooters, in 2008 DeLappe staged a performance that directly merged the real and the virtual: Gandhi's Salt March to Dandi.

On March 12, 2008—the anniversary of Gandhi's historic 1930 protest against the British salt tax—DeLappe began a 386-kilometer virtual march in *Second Life*. His avatar, modeled on Gandhi's likeness, walked step by step across the digital landscape, joined by supporters just as Gandhi had been in India. At the same time, in a New York gallery, DeLappe walked on a treadmill, each step linked in real time to his avatar's progress. The result was a layered performance: part historical reenactment, part endurance art, and part digital protest, dissolving the boundary between physical and virtual space. It was both a homage to Gandhi's Satyagraha (nonviolent resistance) and a reflection on how political activism might be translated into contemporary media.

DeLappe has returned repeatedly to themes of violence, militarism, and memory in his online work. As discussed earlier, his project *Dead-in-Iraq* involved logging into *America's Army*—a military recruitment game designed by the U.S. Army—and typing the names of fallen American soldiers instead of playing. Between 2006 and 2011, he entered 4,484 names, creating a digital cenotaph inside a platform intended to glorify combat.

Another significant project is Elegy: GTA USA Gun Homicides (2018–19). Using the popular open-world crime game *Grand Theft Auto*, DeLappe created a bot-controlled performance in which a character walked through the city randomly killing civilians. The number of murders was calibrated to match the real U.S. gun homicide statistics for 2018—7,293 deaths by July 4th, and over 14,700 by year's end. By visualizing gun deaths through gameplay rather than abstract graphs, DeLappe forced viewers to confront the relentless accumulation of violence in a starkly personal way. What would otherwise be a distant statistic became embodied, one digital death at a time.

COLL.EO: Performance as Digital Reenactment

DeLappe is not alone in using *Grand Theft Auto* as a stage for art. The artist duo COLL.EO (Colleen Flaherty and Matteo Bittanti) has repeatedly used the series to restage performance works from art history.

In *Following Bit* (2012), they reinterpreted Vito Acconci's *Following Piece* (1969). Acconci had randomly selected strangers on the streets of New York, following them for minutes or even hours until they entered a private space.

His goal was to surrender artistic agency to chance and the movements of others, while also probing the boundaries of surveillance and intrusion. COLL.EO transplanted this logic into the digital streets of *Grand Theft Auto*, where their avatar would shadow non-playable characters, mimicking Acconci's gesture but within a coded, algorithmic world. The work raised questions about autonomy, chance, and spectatorship in spaces where "strangers" are programmed rather than free-willed.

Another major project is Liberty City Crawl (2017), inspired by William Pope.L's endurance performances such as *Tompkins Square Crawl* (1991), in which Pope.L crawled through the streets of New York in a suit while holding a potted plant, and *The Great White Way* (2002), where he dragged himself for miles along Broadway in a Superman outfit. COLL.EO's version transposed this action into *GTA's* virtual cityscape, where an avatar crawled endlessly through Liberty City. While Pope.L's original performances highlighted race, class, and physical endurance, the virtual adaptation stripped away the bodily hardship—no sweat, no pain, no dirt—but instead emphasized the symbolic act of crawling in a world designed for speed, violence, and power.

From the Physical Body to the Virtual Avatar

What unites these projects is their translation of historically physical, durational, and often grueling performances into digital environments where embodiment is abstracted through avatars. To crawl on hot asphalt in New York in July, as Pope.L did, is to risk exhaustion and humiliation; to crawl in *GTA* is effortless, detached, and oddly comical. To follow strangers in the street, as Acconci did, is an act of risk and vulnerability; to follow NPCs in a game is a meditation on programmed behavior and surveillance in virtual society.

The shift from body to avatar changes the terms of performance. The absence of sweat, risk, pain, and tactility redefines what is at stake. Yet the questions raised are no less urgent: How do we behave when our bodies are represented digitally? What forms of resistance, endurance, or protest are possible in worlds governed not by physical limits but by coded rules?

Where the 1960s artists tested the limits of flesh, today's digital performers test the limits of simulation. Both traditions challenge audiences to recognize the constructed nature of their environments—whether those environments are the streets of New York, a gallery, or the virtual grids of *Second Life* and *GTA*.

Second Life and Synthetic Performance

The launch of Second Life in 2003 provided artists with a fertile laboratory for performance, economy, and architectural experimentation. Unlike earlier online platforms, Second Life offered open-ended tools for building, scripting, and role-play, which made it especially attractive to artists interested in rethinking presence, embodiment, and community in digital culture.

One of the most influential artist duos to embrace Second Life were Eva and Franco Mattes (0100101110101101.org), whose series *Synthetic Performances* (2007–2010) directly translated canonical works of performance art into the virtual world. Through avatars modeled on their own bodies, they staged digital reenactments of key pieces from the history of performance, including:

- Chris Burden's *Shoot* (1971)
- Vito Acconci's *Seedbed* (1972)
- Valie Export's *Tap and Touch Cinema* (1968–71)
- Marina Abramović and Ulay's *Imponderabilia* (1977)
- Gilbert & George's *The Singing Sculpture* (1969)
- Joseph Beuys' *7000 Oaks* (1982)

These reenactments were not intended as faithful reproductions but as experiments in translation. They asked what happens to works originally dependent on flesh, danger, and intimacy when they are relocated into the coded environment of a virtual world.

Take, for instance, Valie Export's *Tap and Touch Cinema* (1968–71). In the original performance, Export invited passersby to place their hands into a curtained box strapped to her chest, where they could touch her bare torso. The work directly confronted the male gaze, collapsing the distance between cinematic spectatorship and physical intimacy. The shock and unease stemmed from the collision of private touch and public space, forcing participants to reckon with their own desires and taboos.

When reenacted by the Mattes in *Second Life*, the act of touching was no longer bodily but mediated through avatars and mouse clicks. The experience of reaching into a box to touch a living body was replaced by the impersonal mechanics of digital interaction. Yet this disembodiment opened new questions: if nudity and intimacy in Second Life are normalized, does the reenactment still carry any transgressive weight? Or does it instead expose how virtual platforms transform gestures of intimacy into symbolic, almost meaningless exchanges? In this sense, the Mattes' version highlights the loss of tactility and risk in virtual performance while simultaneously critiquing the mechanics of desire in online spaces.

Similarly, Marina Abramović and Ulay's *Imponderabilia* (1977) revolved around the raw presence of bodies in space. In the original performance at the Galleria Comunale d'Arte Moderna in Bologna, the artists stood naked in a narrow doorway, facing one another. Visitors wishing to enter the museum had to squeeze through the gap between their bodies, choosing which performer to face. The work forced an intimate, often uncomfortable confrontation, collapsing the distance between art and audience, and making viewers complicit in the act of performance.

In the Mattes' *Synthetic Performances*, *Imponderabilia* was restaged in Second Life. The artists' avatars stood in a virtual doorway, blocking the passage just as Abramović and Ulay had. But the implications shifted dramatically. Instead of confronting flesh and body heat, viewers encountered pixelated avatars — mutable, customizable bodies that could be walked through, muted, or ignored. The visceral tension of physical proximity was replaced by the mechanics of a rule-based world, where collision detection and avatar boundaries dictate interaction. In this digital translation, the piece becomes less about the vulnerability of naked bodies and more about the conventions of virtual architecture and social codes in online spaces.

In both works, the visceral charge of the original performances is lost in translation, but the Mattes do not treat this as failure. Instead, they embrace the shift, revealing how reenactments in Second Life produce new meanings. By situating historical works of body art in a disembodied, digital environment, the *Synthetic Performances* expose the differences between physical and virtual forms of intimacy, risk, and confrontation.
What emerges is not simply nostalgia for the radicalism of 1970s body art but a new critique: if in the past performance art destabilized the conventions of the gallery and the art audience, in Second Life it destabilizes the conventions of the virtual. The reenactments ask what it means to touch, confront, or protest when the body is no longer flesh but avatar.

This shift mirrors broader questions in contemporary art: how does context redefine meaning? Just as site-specific performances in the 1970s responded to industrial spaces, city streets, or gallery settings, the Second Life reenactments responded to a disembodied, rule-bound environment of the virtual.

The Mattes were not alone. Other artists also discovered Second Life as a stage for hybrid performances such as:

Second Front, a performance art collective founded in 2006 (including members like Jeremy Turner, Liz Solo, and Patrick Lichty), became the first dedicated performance group in Second Life. Their works explored the absurdities and possibilities of virtual embodiment, staging weddings, rituals, and improvisational happenings that referenced Fluxus and Dada traditions.

Cao Fei (China Tracy) created *i.Mirror* (2007), a three-part machinima filmed entirely in Second Life, blending performance, cinema, and documentary. It explored themes of alienation, identity, and the blurring between real and virtual life. Her virtual city *RMB City* (2008–2011) became a platform for performances, exhibitions, and collaborations with international museums.

Gazira Babeli, a "Second Life-born" artist, produced works such as *Gaz of the Desert* (2007), a machinima-performance that critiqued consumerism and spectacle. Her interventions often exploited the malfunctions of the platform itself, creating glitch-based, surreal experiences that paralleled JODI's earlier experiments in game engines.

What unites these practices is a rethinking of the body in a post-physical environment. The discomfort, endurance, and danger central to 1960s and 70s body art were replaced with questions about identity, simulation, and virtual presence. To crawl across Liberty City in *GTA* or to walk Gandhi's march in Second Life is not physically exhausting, but it raises urgent questions about the politics of representation: how do digital bodies perform protest, intimacy, or violence when stripped of material stakes?

In this sense, Second Life became both a stage and a laboratory, continuing the lineage of performance art while simultaneously transforming it. By reenacting historical works, staging new protests, or inventing collective rituals, artists in Second Life highlighted the ways in which performance mutates when mediated by code, avatars, and screens.

The Sims, Parody, and Virtual Lives

Released in 2000 by Maxis, The Sims quickly became one of the best-selling games of its era. Unlike traditional games structured around winning, combat, or quests, *The Sims* offered players an open-ended simulation of everyday life. Players created digital characters, built houses, and guided them through relationships, careers, and domestic routines. Its sandbox structure, life-mirroring mechanics, and potential for emergent chaos made it an unexpected stage for performance art. In this sense, *The Sims* functioned less like a conventional game and more like a virtual theater where artists could script, provoke, or simply observe human behavior.

Artists soon recognized this potential and began experimenting with *The Sims* as a medium for performance:

Rainey Straus and Katherine Isbister's *SimBee* (2004

Rainey Straus and Katherine Isbister's *SimBee* (2004) parodied Vanessa Beecroft's polished, fashion-inflected performances, in which models stand silently in gallery spaces as living sculptures. In *SimBee,* a group of scantily clad Sims were arranged in an immaculate gallery setting. At first, the installation resembled Beecroft's choreographed tableaux, but soon the simulation unraveled. Characters began to act autonomously: they bickered, set fires, collapsed from hunger, or engaged in unexpected outbursts. The work used the game's unstable mechanics to critique Beecroft's tightly controlled aesthetic while also satirizing the unpredictability of both simulated and real social systems. What appeared orderly was always on the verge of collapse.

Caleb Larsen's Simulacrum (2005)

Caleb Larsen's *Simulacrum* (2005) pushed *The Sims* into the realm of autobiographical performance. Larsen painstakingly recreated his apartment, possessions, and daily routines inside the game. For one week, he "lived" as his digital double, documenting the performance through screenshots, blogs, and commentary. The project echoed Allan Kaprow's happenings and the durational endurance works of Tehching Hsieh, collapsing boundaries between game play, life documentation, and performance art. While *SimBee* highlighted chaos, *Simulacrum* explored the uncanny repetition of daily life and the blurring of selfhood across digital and physical domains.

Angela Washko Free Will Mode (2013)

Angela Washko has been one of the most innovative artists to explore *The Sims* (2000), the groundbreaking life-simulation game that offered players a sandbox of domestic life, relationships, and social interaction. Unlike most games of its era, *The Sims* dispensed with linear goals or combat, instead giving players a system for experimenting with everyday routines. For Washko, this environment became a platform for performance, where questions of autonomy, desire, and social coding could be played out in virtual space.

In her series *Free Will Mode* (2013), Washko withdrew direct control over her Sims and allowed their actions to be governed entirely by the game's "free will" setting. What unfolded was a performance shaped not by the artist's hand, but by the algorithmic logic of the software itself. Sims wandered through their homes, pursued relationships, or descended into dysfunction, all according to the game's programmed behavioral scripts. The project reframed *The Sims* as a collaborator, raising questions about how much agency individuals possess within systemic frameworks—digital or social. Just as the Sims are guided by coded needs and invisible constraints, so too are human choices conditioned by cultural, economic, and algorithmic structures.

In *Realistic Fictions* (2013), Washko pushed these explorations further by constructing narratives that exaggerated the game's assumptions about domestic life, gender roles, and romance. By staging Sims in carefully arranged scenarios, she exposed how *The Sims* encodes a very particular vision of suburban middle-class existence, with its emphasis on consumption, heteronormative relationships, and career advancement. The resulting videos oscillate between comedy and critique: while the Sims' melodramatic behaviors often appear absurd, they also reveal the ideological underpinnings of the software.

Together, *Free Will Mode* and *Realistic Fictions* situate Washko's practice at the intersection of performance art, feminist critique, and media studies. Where earlier performance artists tested the boundaries of the body in physical space, Washko investigates how identity and agency are scripted in digital environments. By turning *The Sims* into both stage and subject, she exposes the tension between freedom and control in worlds—virtual or real—where behavior is always mediated by unseen systems.

Mark Beasley's Vito Acconci (The Video Game) (2007)

Some artists go further than modifying existing platforms, building entirely new games to stage performances. Mark Beasley's *Vito Acconci (The Video Game)* (2007), for example, reimagines Acconci's radical performances such as *Seedbed* (1972) and *Following Piece* (1969) as playable scenarios controlled through a Wii remote. In this game, the player does not simply watch Acconci's notorious acts of surveillance or self-exposure—they must perform them. This shift from observer to participant emphasizes the central role of the body and agency in performance art, but it also highlights a core feature of *art games*: they are not designed for entertainment or commercial distribution, but instead use game mechanics to critically investigate cultural, social, or aesthetic questions.

A commonly cited definition of *art games*, first articulated by Rebecca Cannon (2003), describes them as games that are "created to express ideas, rather than to entertain." In this sense, *Vito Acconci (The Video Game)* clearly belongs to the category: it does not reward skill or mastery, but instead uses the structure of a video game to force players into uncomfortable confrontations with performance art's legacy of intimacy, voyeurism, and control.

Pippin Barr's The Artist is Present (2011)

Pippin Barr's *The Artist is Present* (2011) offers another strong example. The game is a minimalist 8-bit simulation of Marina Abramović's durational performance at MoMA, where visitors waited in long lines for the chance to sit silently across from the artist. Barr translates this into a game mechanic centered entirely on waiting, often for hours, before briefly encountering Abramović's pixelated avatar. In conventional games, waiting is framed as wasted time to be minimized; Barr makes it the essence of the experience. This inversion turns the piece into an *art game* because it challenges the expectations of gameplay itself. Instead of entertainment or escape, the game produces reflection on endurance, anticipation, and the construction of meaning through repetition—concerns central to both performance art and contemporary life.

Both works embody why *art games* have become an important category within contemporary art: they employ the formal structures of gaming—rules, interaction, and simulation—not to entertain, but to interrogate history, identity, and culture. By making players into participants in reenacted performances or absurd waiting rooms, Beasley and Barr demonstrate how video games can operate as critical, performative art forms.

Conclusion

Since the 1960s, performance art has consistently sought new arenas beyond the traditional art institution. Where Kaprow and the Fluxus artists took art into the streets, today's digital artists take it into online games, chatrooms, and virtual worlds.

The strategies remain consistent: intervention, reenactment, endurance, parody, participation. But the contexts have changed. In virtual environments, the body is displaced by the avatar, tactility is replaced by code, and risk is redefined not as physical harm but as disruption of the rules of play.

Artists like Joseph DeLappe use performance to rupture the "magic circle" of games and confront players with political realities. Eva and Franco Mattes reanimate the classics of body art in avatar form, probing how meaning shifts in disembodied space. Straus, Isbister, Larsen, Beasley, and Barr show how simulation and participation can generate new kinds of performances that both honor and critique their art-historical predecessors.

In short, online performance art continues the experimental spirit of the 1960s and 70s: it resists commodification, challenges audiences, and insists that art is not a static object but a lived, fleeting encounter—whether in the street, the gallery, or the pixelated space of a game.

Mike Builds a Shelter and Nuclear Games

The early 1980s were a period of heightened global tension, marked by the Cold War's ideological divide and the looming threat of nuclear conflict. Amidst this climate of fear and uncertainty, artists began to explore new mediums to express their concerns and engage the public. One such medium was the emerging field of video games, which, though primarily seen as entertainment, offered a novel platform for artistic and political expression.

The 1980s marked the golden age of home computing and video games. Affordable personal computers like the Commodore 64 (C64), ZX Spectrum, Amstrad CPC, and Apple II brought digital entertainment into people's homes for the first time, transforming how people played, learned, and even created games. These machines were not only gaming platforms but also programming tools, enabling hobbyists to develop their own simple games and experiments.

Mike Builds a Shelter

Mike Builds a Shelter is a pioneering work of video game art created in 1983 by artist Michael Smith, in collaboration with computer graphics designer Dov Jacobson and programmer Reza Keshavarz. It was part of Smith's installation *Government Approved Home Fallout Shelter/Snack Bar*, presented at Castelli Graphics in New York City. The installation featured a custom arcade cabinet housing the game, alongside a mock fallout shelter stocked with survival provisions, records, and liquor bottles—satirizing Cold War-era domestic preparedness.

Gameplay and Concept

In the game, players control a pixelated version of Smith's recurring character, "Mike," who must move three blocks from the first floor of a suburban house to its basement to construct a fallout shelter before an impending nuclear attack. The gameplay is intentionally slow and difficult, with obstacles like fires that can be stamped out but don't affect the player, creating a sense of absurdity and futility. This design choice reflects Smith's critique of the over-simplified and often misguided government preparedness plans of the era.

Artistic and Cultural Significance

Mike Builds a Shelter is considered one of the first art video games, blending the aesthetics and mechanics of early 1980s arcade games with conceptual art. Its satirical approach to Cold War anxieties and domestic life challenges traditional notions of both video games and art. The game was later incorporated into a 1985 video work by Smith, which intersperses Mike's rural adventures with episodes of "Mike's Show" on cable TV, further exploring themes of banality and societal complacency.

Legacy and Restoration

The original arcade cabinet was lost over time, but in 2015, artist and curator Paul Slocum restored *Mike Builds a Shelter* using archival materials and a modernized version of the Commodore 64 hardware. This restoration was showcased at events like the 2014 Frieze Art Fair in London and continues to be exhibited in various art venues

Today, Mike Builds a Shelter is held in the permanent collection of the Museum of Modern Art (MoMA) and is available for educational and screening rentals through Electronic Arts Intermix (EAI).

Artist and video games in the 1980s

While Smith's work was pioneering, he was not alone in exploring the potential of video games for artistic expression during the 1980s. Other artists and designers began to experiment with the medium as:

Jane Veeder's *Warpitout* (1982) stands as a pioneering example of early interactive art games that utilized video game technology to explore themes of identity, self-perception, and the role of the viewer in digital media.

Concept and Gameplay

Warpitout was an interactive installation created by artist Jane Veeder, showcased at the SIGGRAPH '82 Art Show in Boston. The piece was programmed in Zgrass for the Datamax UV-1 graphics computer and housed in a custom arcade-style cabinet. Upon interacting with the installation, participants had their faces digitized and displayed on the screen, where they could manipulate and distort their image using a menu-driven interface. The game featured eight modules that allowed users to apply various graphical effects, resulting in abstract and surreal transformations of their self-portrait. Veeder described the experience as a way to indulge in computer graphics more directly than traditional commercial video games, emphasizing personal expression and interaction over predefined narratives.

Artistic and Political Context

While *Warpitout* did not explicitly address political issues, it emerged during a time of heightened awareness around the role of media and technology in society. The early 1980s saw growing concerns about the impact of digital technologies on personal identity and the potential for media manipulation. By allowing users to distort their own images, *Warpitout* invited reflection on the malleability of identity in the digital age. This aligns with broader artistic movements that questioned the authenticity and representation in media, positioning the work within a critical discourse on technology and society.

Jaron Lanier's *Moondust* (1983) is widely recognized as one of the earliest examples of an "art game," merging interactive gameplay with generative music to create a unique audiovisual experience. Developed for Commodore 64, the game was programmed in 6502 assembly language and published by Creative Software. Its innovative approach to gameplay and music composition has led to its inclusion in various art exhibitions, including the 1983 "ARTcade" at the Corcoran Gallery of Art and the Smithsonian's 2012 "The Art of Video Games".

Gameplay and Mechanics

In *Moondust*, players control a spaceman named Jose Scriabin, named after the synesthetic composer Alexander Scriabin. The objective is to cover a central bullseye with "moonjuice" by dropping seed squares and maneuvering them across the screen. Players must avoid bullet-shaped spaceships while navigating the screen, with their movements influencing the game's abstract ambient soundtrack. The game features four modes: Beginner, Evasive, Freestyle, and Spinsanity, each offering different challenges and control dynamics.

Theatre Europe

The fear of nuclear war also influenced more commercial video games. Released in 1985 by Personal Software Services, *Theatre Europe* was a turn-based strategy game set during a fictional conflict between NATO and the Warsaw Pact. Players controlled military units and made strategic decisions, including the potential use of nuclear weapons. The game's objective was to achieve military dominance while avoiding global annihilation.

What set *Theatre Europe* apart was its incorporation of real-world military data, obtained from the Ministry of Defence and the Soviet embassy in London. This attention to detail lent the game a sense of realism and underscored the gravity of its subject matter. The game also featured a unique mechanic: players were required to call a dedicated telephone number to receive an authorization code for launching nuclear strikes, adding an interactive element that blurred the lines between fiction and reality. *Theatre Europe* received critical acclaim for its accuracy and gameplay, winning the "Best Strategy Game" award at the 1985 Golden Joystick Awards.

WarGames

From the same period is the film *WarGames* (1983) directed by John Badham. The film captures the anxieties of the Cold War era and the growing influence of computers on global security. In the movie, a teenage hacker accidentally accesses a U.S. military supercomputer, almost triggering a nuclear conflict. At first, he believes he has simply discovered a video game and begins interacting with it casually, unaware of the real-world consequences of his actions.

WarGames shares thematic ground with Michael Smith's *Mike Builds a Shelter* (1983) and the 1985 game *Theatre Europe*. Like *Mike Builds a Shelter*, the film reflects public fears of nuclear annihilation, showing how individuals confront the threat in ways both practical and personal. Similarly, *Theatre Europe* places players in the position of military and political decision-makers, forcing them to weigh strategic actions against the potential for catastrophic escalation.

Together, these works illustrate a broader cultural engagement with Cold War anxieties in the early 1980s. Whether through interactive simulation, personal preparation, or cinematic narrative, they invited audiences to grapple with the moral, political, and existential dilemmas posed by the nuclear era.

Legacy and Impact

Both *Mike Builds a Shelter* and *Theatre Europe* exemplify how video games in the 1980s were used as platforms for political and artistic expression. They demonstrated that games could engage players in critical reflection on societal issues, using interactivity to deepen the impact of their messages.

These early works laid the groundwork for the evolution of today's serious games and art games, which aim to educate, train, persuade, or raise awareness about real-world issues. They combine interactive gameplay with meaningful content, often engaging players in learning, problem-solving, or critical thinking.

These games later influenced artists and game designers who continued to explore the medium's potential for storytelling and social commentary. Today, video games are increasingly recognized as a legitimate form of artistic expression, with institutions like the Museum of Modern Art in New York exhibiting works that showcase the medium's artistic and cultural significance.

War, Refugees, and Videogames: From Space Invaders to Contemporary Artistic Interventions

The evolution of war-themed video games reflects not only technological advancements but also shifting cultural attitudes toward conflict, violence, and human suffering. From the pixelated alien invaders of *Space Invaders* (1978) to the hyper-realistic first-person shooters (FPS) of today, games have increasingly simulated complex, immersive theaters of war, often mirroring contemporary geopolitical anxieties. While early arcade games abstracted conflict into simple mechanics, modern titles frequently grapple with realism, strategy, and moral consequence, offering both players and observers a lens to interrogate the ethics and aesthetics of warfare. In parallel, a growing number of artists have appropriated these digital war environments to examine human suffering, displacement, and the socio-political dimensions of conflict.

The earliest war-inspired games, like *Space Invaders* and *Missile Command* (1980), treated conflict as a mechanical challenge: waves of enemies descending from the sky or missiles threatening cities. These games coincided with Cold War anxieties, often abstracting nuclear threat into simplistic, easily digestible scenarios. As technology evolved, titles like *Call of Duty* and *Battlefield* brought historical and modern warfare into hyper-realistic first-person perspectives, creating immersive simulations that replicate the sensory experience of battle. These games foreground not just tactics and reflexes but the affective experience of soldiers, civilians, and the chaos of conflict zones. Within this context, contemporary artists have leveraged these platforms to critique and reframe the portrayal of war and its human toll.

Games like *Call of Duty* and *Medal of Honor* have often worked closely with military consultants to ensure authenticity, reinforcing narratives of Western military heroism. However, this close relationship has also sparked criticism, especially when games sanitize or glorify conflict without addressing its human cost.

This blurring of entertainment and propaganda has led scholars to describe the phenomenon as the "military–entertainment complex," where games, films, and media collaborate to shape public perception of war.

Joseph DeLappe's "dead-in-iraq" (2006–2011)

Joseph DeLappe is a pioneering figure in the intersection of digital art, political activism, and video game performance. One of his most powerful and widely recognized works is "dead-in-iraq" (2006–2011), a long-running intervention within the U.S. Army's online recruitment game *America's Army*. This project exemplifies how video games can be repurposed as platforms for dissent, remembrance, and critique.

America's Army is a free-to-play first-person shooter developed by the U.S. military as both a recruitment tool and a training simulator. With millions of downloads, it became a central part of the military–entertainment complex, offering young players a sanitized and gamified version of military life. DeLappe's intervention subverted this narrative by introducing the harsh reality of war into the game's virtual space.

Using the in-game chat system—normally reserved for tactical communication—DeLappe entered the names, ages, and dates of death of U.S. soldiers killed in the Iraq

War. He did this under the username "dead-in-iraq", refusing to participate in gameplay. Instead, he stood motionless, typing names while other players engaged in combat around him. His avatar was routinely shot, but he would respawn and continue the memorial.

This act transformed the game into a digital vigil. By juxtaposing real-world death with virtual violence, DeLappe forced players to confront the human cost of war in a space designed to obscure it. The performance blurred the line between entertainment and mourning, turning a recruitment tool into a site of resistance and remembrance

Velvet Strike (2002–2003)

Similarly, collective interventions such as *Velvet Strike* (2002–2003) illustrate how artists and activists can leverage the modding capabilities of commercial video games to challenge dominant political narratives. Conceived by the artists Anne-Marie Schleiner, Joan Leandre and Brody Condon, *Velvet Strike* emerged in direct response to U.S. military actions in Afghanistan and Iraq. Using the popular FPS *Counter-Strike* as a platform, the project transformed ordinary maps into sites of virtual protest: players could spray graffiti messages such as "Make Love Not War" or other anti-militarist slogans onto the game's architecture, converting spaces designed for competitive combat into canvases for political expression.

The project was deliberately ephemeral, reflecting both the transient nature of online play and the urgency of its political critique. By subverting the game's mechanics—turning a tool for simulated violence into one for communication and dissent—*Velvet Strike* highlighted the potential of player agency as a form of resistance, demonstrating that digital environments could serve as arenas for social and cultural critique rather than mere entertainment.

Eddo Stern's Vietnam Romance (2003)

Vietnam Romance is a long-form art game and multimedia installation by Eddo Stern that interrogates the cultural memory and commodification of the Vietnam War. At its core, *Vietnam Romance* is a remix of the Vietnam War experience, constructed entirely from digital artifacts—video game clips, MIDI soundtracks, and stylized graphics. The game's slogan, "If you hated the War but liked the Movies, you'll love this Game," sets the tone for its ironic and critical stance. It invites players into a surreal, side-scrolling diorama that feels more like a playable collage than a conventional video game.

Visually, *Vietnam Romance* is striking. Stern uses hand-painted watercolors, digitally processed into 3D models, to create a tactile, dreamlike environment. This aesthetic choice distances the player from realism, emphasizing the constructed nature of war memories and the artificiality of their representation in games and films. The result is a playable space that feels like a nostalgic scrapbook—beautiful, haunting, and deeply ironic

The game's soundtrack, composed of MIDI versions of 1960s pop songs, further blurs the line between reality and fiction. These familiar tunes evoke both the era of the war and its cinematic retellings, reinforcing the idea that our understanding of Vietnam is mediated through entertainment. Stern's use of machinima and game assets from titles like *Deer Hunter*, *Platoon*, and *Vietcong* underscores how war has been gamified and aestheticized to the point of abstraction

Stern's project is not just a critique of the Vietnam War's portrayal—it's a broader reflection on how war becomes myth through repetition, commodification, and digital simulation. By inviting players to "Feel the Nam, Feel the elephant grass, Feel the red clay, Feel the cong," the game mocks the immersive language of war games and tourism, exposing the absurdity of trying to "experience" war through pixels and nostalgia.

Contemporary Conflicts: Ukraine and Palestine

In the wake of Russia's invasion of Ukraine in 2022, artists and collectives have continued to use video games as spaces for protest, solidarity, and critical reflection. The ubiquity of online platforms, streaming, and modding has opened up new avenues for anti-war expression that echo earlier interventions but are deeply tied to the geopolitics of the present.

Total Refusal How to Disappear (2020)

The Austrian collective Total Refusal—sometimes called the "pseudo-marxist media guerilla"—has produced machinima works that repurpose commercial war games into anti-war films. In *How to Disappear* (2020), made with *Battlefield V*, the group highlights the act of desertion rather than combat, following avatars who refuse to fight. By refusing the logic of battle in a game designed for military heroism, the project opens a poetic space for pacifism, futility, and resistance within hyper-militarized environments. Their films have circulated widely in art and film festivals, situating game-based performance within a global discourse of protest.

Other artists have turned to game modification as a tool of solidarity. In 2022, Ukrainian developers and modders created content within titles like *Minecraft* and *Arma 3* to document the destruction of cultural landmarks or to simulate the defense of Ukrainian cities. While some of these projects veer toward propaganda or morale-boosting, artists have critically engaged with these same spaces to question the aesthetics of war tourism, the dangers of gamifying real violence, and the thin line between documentation and spectacle.

Rasheed Abueideh's Liyla and the Shadows of War (2016)

Beyond Ukraine, artists from conflict regions have also mobilized games to express civilian experiences of war. Palestinian developer Rasheed Abueideh's *Liyla and the Shadows of War* (2016) remains a key precedent: a minimalist platformer in which players must make impossible decisions under bombardment. Similarly, Joseph DeLappe's collaborative project *Killbox* (2016), developed with the Biome Collective, simulates drone warfare over northern Iraq, forcing players to inhabit both the perspectives of remote pilots and local victims. These projects extend the tradition of *Velvet-Strike* and *dead-in-iraq* by demonstrating that video games are not neutral spaces but contested terrains where narratives of violence, victimhood, and resistance collide.

In the contemporary moment, war games have become not just entertainment or recruitment tools but stages for artistic intervention, remembrance, and activism. From desertion machinima to refugee storytelling, artists continue to reframe the digital battlefield as a space of empathy, critique, and resistance—reminding us that in an era where war itself is increasingly mediated through screens, the struggle over representation is as urgent as ever.

Refugees, Borders, and Video Games

Alongside direct critiques of military violence, artists have also used video games to address the plight of refugees and the politics of borders. These works shift the focus from battlefields to the lived experience of displacement, incarceration, and migration, demonstrating how game mechanics can become powerful metaphors for systemic oppression.

Escape from Woomera (2003)

One of the earliest and most influential projects in this field is *Escape from Woomera* (2003), developed by a collective of Australian artists and activists. The game was based on the real-life Woomera Immigration Reception and Processing Centre, a remote detention camp for asylum seekers in South Australia. Built on the *Half-Life* engine, the project placed players in the position of detainees attempting to escape confinement. Unlike conventional shooters, the game did not emphasize combat but instead survival, restriction, and the impossibility of freedom within carceral systems. Its release sparked significant controversy in Australia, where critics accused it of trivializing a sensitive issue, while supporters hailed it as an innovative example of political art that gave visibility to silenced voices.

Darfur is Dying (2006)

Is one of the earliest and most widely circulated "serious games" to address the refugee experience. Developed by a team of students at the University of Southern California in collaboration with humanitarian organizations, the browser-based game placed players in the role of a displaced Darfuri villager living in a refugee camp. The central mechanic involved leaving the safety of the camp to collect water, while avoiding the threat of roaming militias. By combining simple gameplay with the constant risk of capture or death, the game translated the precarious daily struggles of refugees into an interactive form accessible to a broad online audience. Reaching millions of players worldwide, *Darfur is Dying* demonstrated how video games could function as tools of advocacy and awareness, using play to foster empathy for distant humanitarian crises often reduced to statistics in the news.

Italiani Brava Gente (1996)

The concept of politically engaged video games is not new. As early as 1996, Italian artist Antonio Riello created *Italiani Brava Gente*, repurposing the classic arcade shooter format to deliver a sharp political critique. In the game, players must intercept and destroy boats carrying Albanian refugees approaching Italian shores, reflecting how politicians and media often framed immigration as an "invasion." The ironic title—"Italians Are Good People"—questions whether Italian society truly lived up to that self-image. Widely recognized as one of the earliest examples of a politically engaged or "serious" game, *Italiani Brava Gente* uses interactivity to challenge nationalist sentiment and make players confront their own complicity in real-world narratives of exclusion.

Conclusion

From the early abstractions of *Space Invaders* to contemporary immersive simulations, video games have both reflected and shaped cultural understandings of war. Artists have harnessed these digital spaces to critique militarism, humanize conflict, and highlight the experiences of civilians and refugees, transforming games from tools of entertainment or propaganda into platforms for reflection and activism. Works such as Joseph DeLappe's *Dead-in-Iraq*, Velvet-Strike, Eddo Stern's *Vietnam Romance, Escape from Woomera*, and Antonio Riello's *Italiani Brava Gente* demonstrate the power of interactivity to confront players with the ethical, emotional, and political dimensions of conflict. Together, these interventions reveal that video games are not neutral mirrors of war—they are contested spaces where art can expose, question, and reimagine the realities of violence, displacement, and human resilience.

Game Art Exhibitions a summary

Game Art exhibitions over the past 25 years trace the intersection of contemporary art and video games, showing how artists have used games as platforms for creativity, critique, and cultural exploration.

In the mid-1990s, early projects like Orhan Kipcak's *Arsdoom* at Ars Electronica 1995 used the *Doom* engine to create immersive artistic environments. Similarly, Palle Torsson and Tobias Bernstrup's *Museum Meltdown* (Arken Museum, 1996) repurposed first-person shooter (FPS) mechanics to critique art institutions, signaling the beginnings of a dialogue between game engines and contemporary art. These works treated FPS technology not merely as entertainment but as a tool for conceptual experimentation.

By the late 1990s, modding culture became central. Exhibitions such as *Synreal: The Unreal Modification* (1998) and Anne-Marie Schleiner's *Cracking the Maze* (1999) showcased artists like JODI, Axel Stockburger, and Natalie Bookchin hacking *Quake* and *Unreal Tournament* maps, creating glitch aesthetics and interactive interventions. These works exemplified how FPS engines could be transformed into playable artworks, exploring narrative, space, and player agency while reflecting contemporary art's interest in interactivity, appropriation, and networked culture.

The early 2000s saw institutional recognition. Exhibitions like *SHIFT-CTRL: Computers, Games & Art* (2000) and *Game Show* (2001, Mass MoCA) brought works created in engines like *Half-Life* and *Quake* mods into museum spaces. Cory Arcangel's experiments with *Super Mario Bros.* and Feng

Mengbo's *Q4U* combined technical ingenuity with cultural critique, showing how FPS and platformer mechanics could become a medium for storytelling and political commentary.

From the mid-2000s, exhibitions such as *Game/Play* (2006, UK), *Next Level* (Stedelijk Museum, Amsterdam), and *Breaking and Entering* (Pace Wildenstein, NY) highlighted the diversity of game-based practice. Artists worked with *Quake*, *Unreal Tournament*, and custom engines to explore public space, identity, and social networks, while machinima and modding extended the FPS vocabulary into narrative and performative art. Global interest in Game Art grew alongside the rise of online gaming and user-generated content, showing a convergence of technical and artistic innovation.

In the 2010s and beyond, Game Art exhibitions like *Art and Videogames Neoludic* (Venice Biennale, 2011), *Open World* (Akron Art Museum, 2019), and *WORLDBUILDING* (Julia Stoschek Collection, 2022–23) showcased sophisticated uses of FPS engines, procedural generation, and VR. Artists such as Ian Cheng, LaTurbo Avedon, Cory Arcangel, and Cao Fei created immersive environments blending installation, performance, and interactivity. FPS-derived mechanics—movement, navigation, and first-person perspective—became tools for engaging audiences in critical reflection, narrative exploration, and aesthetic experimentation.

Across this trajectory, Game Art exhibitions reveal how FPS technology, modding culture, and contemporary art practice grew together. From early Doom and Quake mods to immersive VR and procedural game worlds, video games evolved from playful experiments into recognized contemporary art forms, demonstrating the power of engines and mods to transform interactivity, space, and cultural critique into a legitimate artistic language.

Reference books about Game Art

- "Game Art Around the World: From Japan to Cuba" (jag behöver inget förlag, 2015), ISBN 9789186915193. *Comment: A collection of interviews I did with artists creating Game Art.*
- "The Pioneers of Game Art: From ArsDoom to SimBee", (jag behöver inget förlag, 2015), ISBN 9789186915186. *Comment: A collection of interviews I did with the pioneers of Game Art.*
- "Everything I Shoot Is Art", Mathias Jansson, ISBN 9781291020502, Link Editions, 2012. *Comment: A collection of texts I wrote about Game Art in different magazines and blogs.*
- "When Art Is Put Into Play: A Practice-based Research Project on Game Art" Arne Kjell Vikhagen, diss 2017 University of Gothenburg. Faculty of Fine, Applied and Performing Arts. *Comment: A dissertation about Game Art written by artist and researcher Vikhagen.*
- "Videogames and Art" by Andy Clarke (Editor), Grethe Mitchell (Editor), (Intellect, 2014, Second edition), ISBN 978-1-84150-419-3, 260 pages. *Comment: This new and revised edition features an extended critical introduction from the editors and updated interviews with the foremost artists in the field.*
- "Works of Game: On the Aesthetics of Games and Art", Johan Sharp, (The MIT Press, 2015), ISBN 978-0262029070. *Comment: About Game Art and art game with artists like Julian Oliver, Cory Arcangel, JODI, etc.*

- "Gamescenes: Art in the Age of Videogame" by Matteo Bittanti and Domenico Quarant, (john & Levi, 2006), ISBN 88-6010-010-0, 456 pages. *Comment: Some short essays and an impressive catalogue about Game Art artists and their works.*
- "Unstable Aesthetics: Game Engines and the Strangeness of Modding" by Eddie Lohmeyer, (Bloomsbury Academic, 2023), ISBN 978-1501374708, 216 pages. *Comment: About modding game engines mention artists such as Cory Arcangel, JODI, Julian Oliver.*
- "At the Edge of Art" by Joline Blais and Jon Ippolito, (Thames & Hudson, 2006), ISBN 978-0500238226, 256 pages. *Comment: Pages 57-91 are about Game Art, artists like Eddo Stern, John Klima, Natalie Bookchin, Eric Zimmerman.*
- "Digital Art" by Christiane Paul (Thames & Hudson, 2003), ISBN 0-500-20367-9, 224 pages. *Comment: Pages 196-203 is about Game Art, artists such as Natalie Bookchin, JODI, Cory Archangel, Feng Mengbo.*
- "New Media Art" by Mark Tribe/Reena Jana (Taschen, 2006), ISBN 3-8228-3041-0, 100 pages. *Comment: Game Art works as Cory Arcangels "Super Mario Clouds", Natalie Bookchin "The Intruder" and Schleiner, Leandro and Condons "Velvet Strike" are described in the book.*
- "Internet Art" by Rachel Greene (Thames & Hudson, 2004), ISBN 0-500-20376-8, 224 pages. *Comment: Pages 144-151 is about Game Art, artists like*

Natalie Bookchin, Brody Condon, Eddo Stern, Thomson and Craighead etc.
- "Space Time Play: Computer Games, Architecture and Urbanism: The Next Level", ed. Friedrich von Borres and Steffen P.Walz, (Birkhauser, 2007), ISBN 978-3-7643-8414-2, 495 pages. *Comment: Mainly about the relationship between games and architechture, but also some examples such as Blinkenlights and other more artistic games.*
- "From Sun Tzu to Xbox War and Video Games" by Ed Halter, (Thunder's Mouth Press, 2006), ISBN 1560256818. *Comment: Ed Halter tells the story of War and computer games. At the end of the book, he mentions artists like "The Velvet Strike team", Johan Klima, Eddo Stern etc.*
- "Gaming: Essays on Algorithmic Culture" by Alexander R. Galloway, (Univ.Minnesota P., 2006), ISBN 0816648514. *Comment: Tells the history of the origins of the FPS. A chapter is called "Countergaming" about Artist-Made Game Mods.*
- "Persuasive Games: The Expressive Power of Videogames" by Ian Bogost, (The MIT Press, 2007), ISBN 978-0-262-02614-7. *Comment: Chapter "Digital Democracy" p.121-141 includes works as Velvet-Strike, 9-11 survivor, Waco Resurrection by C-Level.*
- "Critical Play: Radical Game Design" Mary Flanagan, (The MIT Press, 2009), ISBN 9780262062688. *Comment: Chapter "Critical Computer Games" about Game Art as Natalie Bookchin, Eddo Stern, Wafaa Bilal.*

- "New Media in the White Cube and Beyond", ed. Christiane Paul, (University of California Press, 2008), ISBN 978-0-520-25597-5. Comment: *Pages 233-250, Tilman Baumgärtel writes about the exhibition "Games: Computer Games by Artist" and the early history of Game Art.*
- "SwanQuake: the user manual" (2007) by Scott deLahunta (Editor), Bruno Martelli & Ruth Gibson (Author), ISBN 978-1841021720. Comment: *About the artwork Swanquake and Game Art in general.*
- "The Rendered Arena: Modalities of Space in Video and Computer Games", (2009), by Axel Stockburger, ISBN 978-3639207767. Comment: *Axel Stockburgers thesis about spatiality in videogames and art.*
- "Artists Re: Thinking Games", (2010), by Ruth Catlow (Author, Editor), Marc Garrett (Editor), Corrado Morgana (Editor), ISBN 978-1846312472.

www.ingramcontent.com/pod-product-compliance
Lightning Source LLC
Chambersburg PA
CBHW070309230526
45470CB00002B/787